HOMO SAPIENS

All rights reserved
Shimon Garber
TX 8-821-907

©2019

All rights reserved. No part of this book may be
reproduced in form or by means—whether electronic, digital, mechanical,
or otherwise—without permission in writing from the publisher, except by a
reviewer, who may quote brief passages in a review.

Unless specified, all Scripture is taken from the New King James Version®.
Copyright © 1982 by Thomas Nelson. It has been used with permission.
All rights reserved.

Translate by Shimon Garber
Russian Text Editor: Anna Pelan
Russian Text Corrector: Era
Designer: Tom Howey
Publisher: Newcomers Authors Publishing Group

HS I-II 978-1950430345; HC
HS I-II 978-1950430352; Epub
HS III 978-1950430369; HC
HS III 978-1950430376; Epub

2023

Shimon Garber

HOMO SAPIENS

VOL I & II

A collection of essays

SUPERSTITION • FAITH • RELIGION • POLITICS

SECOND EDITION

CONTENTS

VOLUME I

Preface	9
Who Are We?	15
How It All Began	19
Homo Sapiens	21
Our Ancestors	25
Totems and Taboos	30
Religion	34
The First Civilizations	37
Sumerian Social Society	41
New Religion	43
Persians	50
Monotheism	55
The Maccabees' Rebellion	55
Christianity	58
Islam	68
Religion and Civilization	70
The Rights of the Strongest	72
The Later Middle Ages	74
Discovery of America	77
Democracy	82
Europe in the Twentieth Century	86

Social Democratic Movements	89
Europe After World War II	97
European Union	99
USA and Radical Democrats	102
Meet Hillary Clinton	115
The Clinton Foundation	122
Ideologies	126
New-Old Religion: Democracy	133

VOLUME II

Preface	157
Beginning	160
Brain and Evolution	163
Duality of Consciousness	172
The Evolution of Homo Sapiens	178
Conquering the Planet	185
Knowledge and Faith	191
The Negative Aspects of Religion	202
Democracy in the United States	211
Coronavirus	253
Consequences of the Coronavirus Pandemic	273

PREFACE

The questions of the universe, humanity, and its place on Earth appear in any thinking person's mind. The Universal Declaration of Human Rights states: *All people are born free and equal.*

The Founding Fathers of America envisaged almost everything. But even they could not have foreseen that society would change so much. Differently thinking people have come to power through democratic elections. People with contrasting ideas to the Founding Fathers on freedom, good, and evil have become the majority. They seek to tax everything and spend it to change the world. Democrats have gone from defending slavery to promoting socialism and are moving further to the left. They want to lower the age limit of voters to sixteen and give illegal immigrants and felons the right to vote. For the sake of power, they are ready to change the Constitution radically.

The ideology, though I prefer the word *religion*, of communism has once again reared its ugly head, and the uneducated citizens demand the redistribution of wealth throughout general society.

All people are born equal and free. That is true in one sense. But I always thought this statement was somewhat naive and pathetic because some people are born healthy and wealthy, while others are poor and sick. There are persistent inequalities. Wise and not so bright. Lucky and unfortunate. Some are born in an ethical and free country. Others are born in terrible third-world countries with no freedom and no food. Some have loving families where the children are loved and cherished. Others live in unhappy families where children are seen as a burden. The divisions are endless.

Social inequalities meet us from the day of our birth and accompany us throughout our life journey: racial, national, gender, physical, intellectual, and social. Our unique talents, demographics, birthplace, and many other factors affect our lives.

Some receive dividends from inherited wealth or gains made by their efforts; others live day to day through the sweat of their brow. Also, some cannot work, and some do not wish to work.

All these social inequalities have led to the stratification of society. Today, less fortunate people in the social hierarchy, mostly from minority groups, are gaining now more government seats. Their voices are getting louder and more demanding. The freedoms, for which these minorities have fought for many years are now a reality. We cannot turn back time and undo mistakes that were made.

All these groups are becoming the majority of the population; our planet's future is in their hands. It is up to our descendants to deal with it, for better or worse. They must go down this unexplored path. We do not know whether they will defend traditional values or invent others.

What awaits our society tomorrow? Civil war, chaos, or something even worse? As we leave, we wish them good luck and pray for them: everyone, even nonbelievers.

"Hell is full of good meanings and wishes."
GEORGE HERBERT

WHO ARE WE?

From the moment of self-awareness, we ask ourselves questions like, who am I? Who created me? Who created this world, scary and hostile?

The Torah (the first five books in the Judeo-Christian Bible as Old Testament) in Judaism offers an explanation of the origin of the universe and all that exists on this Earth: "The Earth was without form and void, and darkness was on the face of the deep. And the Spirit of God was hovering over the face of the waters." (Gen. 1:2).

The Creator was bored and decided to make something glorious. For the following six days, the Creator worked extremely hard. Of course, He was in the process of making everything. God saw that the Earth was such a pretty and spacious place. On the sixth day, the Creator made a man in his image and likeness and then a woman from man's rib.

On the seventh day, the Creator rested. The newlyweds inhabited Mesopotamia's area between the rivers Tigris and Euphrates, where the Garden of Eden was at that time. Adam and Eve broke the Creator's direct order: do not eat from the tree of knowledge that grew in the middle of the garden.

The woman gave the fruit to her husband, who also ate it, and they were banished forever from the Garden of Eden. Thus began the history of suffering and torment of the entire human race.

For centuries, these narrations of biblical history have been a simple explanation of people's origins, but not for everyone. Curious people have searched for the correct answers to many questions for millennia. How was the universe created? When did it happen? From where did the first human come? How was humanity able to spread all over the planet? Where was the cradle of humanity, and when did it happen?

Different religious beliefs have been expressed at different times. In ancient, unenlightened centuries for any heretical statements, it was relatively easy to get cleansing at inquisitions' bonfires. Even in old times, some advanced scientists thought about the evolutionary development of humanity. In the nineteenth through twenty-first centuries, new information on human evolution spread. Literature, art, science, archeology, genetics, and paleontology brought down on not-quite-prepared humans' heads such an avalanche of information that all humans did not know before.

Everything that had been cherished throughout human history suddenly collapsed. As Russian poet A. Pushkin wrote in his *Epistle to Siberia*: "The heavy fetters will fall,/ The dungeons will collapse, and freedom / Will receive you joyfully at the entrance."

Freedom from what? From knowledge of ancient and cherished religions? From history, astronomy, physics, history?

Who were our ancestors who sought such freedom? It turns out that everything was dark then. Even now, we still argue about our ancestors. What about knowledge, art, literature, music, painting, sculpture, and philosophy? Back then, the best minds and talents created masterpieces, recorded the most profound revelations of human thoughts, and stood up for what they believed, even going to death. In dark cells with small candles, they described the universe and the most profound revelations of human feelings.

We pondered and debated the cornerstones of human existence: truth, faith, hope, virtue, justice, and supreme power, with its giving and punishing power. What is the meaning of being, and what is its end? What is accurate, and what is illusory?

The modern interpretation of the universe's processes has spread worldwide through mass media, scientists' treatises, nonfiction literature, and, most relevant today, social media. With computer-generated graphics, we have created genuinely epic pictures of the universe's nature and a history of human evolution, further developing the first and subsequent civilizations on Earth.

We are armed with knowledge about our ancestors and how they survived those harsh conditions and even multiplied so much that they inhabited the entire globe. Reality could never be more joyful than fairy tales, beliefs, an expectation of a miracle power of fate, and hope for a reward for obedience, virtue, and justice. Has life become more fun? Let's turn to the famous Russian poet M. Lermontov's words on the death of A. Pushkin: "There's a formidable judgment that's waiting; He does not have greed for the gold, and he knows the thoughts and deeds upfront."

The faith in retribution and justice did help humankind survive the most painful and bitter blows of fate.

HOW IT ALL BEGAN

Time goes by, and now we hear new theories about Big Bang. As we know, our Earth is already an old lady. About 13.8 billion years ago, a small clot of matter exploded and began to expand and thus spawning our entire universe. We called it the Big Bang.

Planet Earth appeared 4.5 billion years ago from cosmic dust and gas. Perhaps it resembled the sun or Saturn with dust rings. Without an atmosphere, Earth was bombarded by space objects. One such collision led to a tilt of the Earth's axis and the moon's formation.

There are different theories about how water appeared on Earth. Water condenses to give us clouds, which create a protective atmosphere and make it habitable for living organisms. Over billions of years, the land has cooled down and acquired a thick crust. About 580 million years ago, multicellular life took hold. Those organisms arose and evolved or died out. Glacial periods, changing climatic conditions, tectonic plate shifts, volcanic activity, and collisions with asteroids altered the planet's appearance and forced living organisms to adapt to changing circumstances. The Jurassic Period began about 200 million years ago and lasted 56 million years. The real lords of the Earth were dinosaurs. Humans did not exist at that time. Sixty-five million years ago, the Earth collided with a giant meteorite at the end of the Cretaceous Period. The consequences were catastrophic. Dinosaurs and many other reptiles were erased from the face of Earth, making way for mammals.

HOMO SAPIENS

The climate in Africa about three million years ago was much wetter than today. The conditions favored rich plant and animal diversity. Tall trees allowed primates to live on trees and eat leaves and some berries without fear of predators. The climate changed, and trees became smaller and sparser. There were some different opinions about the environment in Africa at that time. Some scientists said the climate got warmer and wetter with many lakes and rivers. It attracted birds and various small aquatic inhabitants. Primates had to go down to the ground and travel distances, looking for food. Because they had to go into the water, searching for food, they had to stand straight up on their hind legs. They learned to find edible protein from small aquatic creatures. In addition to birds' eggs and remnants of meat left by predators, they could also eat leftover meat abandoned by predators or the flesh of other primates and small animals they could catch. These new living conditions led to changes in their bodies. Eating meat contributed to an increase in the size of their brains. They learned to hunt together, which required coordination and the exchange of sounds to communicate. To kill and share food with other clan members, they had to learn how to use stone and stick tools. Over time, this collaborative thinking and some types of speaking primates became the first humanoids.

Charles R. Darwin (1809–1882), an English naturalist and traveler, was the first to promote the idea that all living organisms evolved and originated from common ancestors. In his 1851 book, *On the Origin of Species,* he revolutionized the field of natural history and refuted the belief in the divine origin of humans, and questioned belief and religion itself.

Charles Darwin's theory caused a storm of indignation. He was considered a precursor to the Antichrist, but some people compared him to Aristotle and Newton. Darwin, however, was not the first scholar to contradict the teachings of the Church. The following scientists and thinkers opposed the conventional thinking of their day.

Copernicus (1473–1543) described the model of the world, placing the sun in the center of our universe. His work, *About the Rotation of Celestial Spheres,* published in the sixteenth century, offered a new model of the world where the sun is the center of the universe and planets move around it.

Galileo Galilei (1564–1642) was the inventor of the telescope, accused by the Church of heresy and was placed under house arrest for the rest of his life.

Giordano Bruno (1548–1600) was convicted as a heretic and sentenced to death by burning.

Isaac Newton (1643–1727) was a physicist, mathematician, astronomer, historian, and alchemist. His second work, *Mathematical Beginnings of Natural Philosophy*, laid out the law of global gravity.

Not many people today doubt that *Homo sapiens* came from hominids. Modern scientists agree on new dating of hominids splitting from apes, and following their own evolutionary path, to about ten million years ago. Congrats to all racists and others who care about the purity of race.

Now we have a theory about the origin of our species, *Homo sapiens*. We know that humanity comes not only from Africa. To date, it is already known about the discovery of the remains of a hybrid of Neanderthals and *Homo sapiens*, who lived about 30-40 thousand years ago in Riparo di Mezzena (northern Italy). The same remains were found in Crimea (Staroselie). Crossings of Neanderthals and Cro-Magnons (modern people), Neanderthals and Denisovans, and Cro-Magnons and Denisovans are genetically confirmed.

In 2010, the remains of other extinct *Homo species* were identified. Denisovans (*Homo altaiensis*), an unknown population of hominids found in the Denisovskaya Cave, northwest of the Russian Altai. The remains belonged to a species of people previously unknown to science. Before this, it was believed that only two types of people inhabited Eurasia—the Neanderthals and the Cro-Magnons who came after them (the ancestors of *Homo sapiens*). Genetic analysis showed that the new species (the Denisovan man) was close to the Neanderthals but diverged from them along different branches of evolution about 640,000 years ago.

The remains of an extinct form of hominids, named Dmanisi hominid, were found on the territory of Georgia, formerly known as *Homo erectus georgicus*. Ancient sites of the first hominids are found on the territory of Kazakhstan.

OUR ANCESTORS

Africa is now recognized as the main cradle of humanity. 2.5 million-year-old remains of a human ancestors named *Lucy* were discovered in Ethiopia, Africa. Lucy was an Australopithecus, an extinct hominid that could be related to *Homo sapiens*. It was the earliest species of humanoid creature known at the time. Anthropologists later found the skeleton of a 3.5 million-year-old Australopithecus. It was short, standing only about three feet tall, and had much less brain volume than humans today, about four hundred cubic centimeters. The last humanoid skeleton found in West Africa dates from seven million years ago. It walked on two legs but most likely did not speak. The first hominids dwelt at the tops of trees and only went to the ground to collect fruits, grass, and leaves. They probably lived in clans. The genus *Homo* was the next step in developing the hominids and was more skillful than the Australopithecus.

Homo habilis lived about 2.5 million years ago. They walked on two legs and probably made stone tools. The next step in the evolutionary process was the upright man, *Homo erectus*, or Pithecanthropus. According to *Encyclopedia Britannica*, they lived about two million years ago and had low, sloping foreheads and a brain volume of about a thousand cubic centimeters. Somewhere between the Australopithecus and the Neanderthal man, hominids started using fire. They are now extinct.

Homo neanderthalensis lived about 400,000 years ago to around 30,000 years ago. Their brain volume corresponded to *Homo sapiens* at approximately 1,600 cubic centimeters, and their foreheads were a little more prominent. Anthropologists have found traces of some culture at Neanderthal sites. Ritual objects and cave paintings suggest they migrated from Africa about two million years ago and inhabited Eurasia.

Some scientists believe that Neanderthals are a dead-end branch of evolution. Some scientists believe their genes are still more extant in some populations than in others.

The genes Cro-Magnons (*Homo sapiens sapiens*) appeared in Europe and modern France about fifty thousand to forty thousand years ago. They left numerous artifacts, such as cave paintings, miniature sculptures, jewelry, and more. Cro-Magnon sites suggest they had somewhat increased the development of culture. *Homo sapiens* inhabited all of Earth fifty thousand to forty thousand years ago.

Africa's changing climate forced hunter-gatherer societies to seek new habitats. The first human migration began about two million years ago. *Homo erectus* was followed by the Cro-Magnons. They appeared in the Near East about 100,000 years ago. There the streams split. Some went to Asia Minor and from there to Europe.

Others went south and east. Some moved further to South Asia and East to India and China.

When *Homo sapiens* arrived in Europe, they found Neanderthals, who had already lived there for one hundred thousand to sixty thousand years. *Homo sapiens* were fitter for surviving the conditions. They were armed with lighter spears than Neanderthals and could throw them farther. Some theories suggest that *Homo sapiens* killed Neanderthals and probably ate them. It was typical among early men to celebrate victory over the enemy by eating their flesh and brain. It showed a sense of superiority and was thought to be a way to gain the enemy's strength. Such a repast meant the complete triumph of the family and promoted a closer association.

It could be that some social contact existed, maybe not voluntary. *Homo sapiens* inhabited almost the entire landmass of the world. The Neanderthals died out, and *Homo sapiens* inherited 3 percent of their genes.

I knew a submarine captain who looked like a Neanderthal. He was a most excellent man. He was short, with a massive body and excessive woolly hair. We knew nothing about Neanderthals and called him a Challenger, a character from Arthur Conan Doyle's book *The Lost World*.

The Earth's last Ice Age was around twelve thousand years ago. The glaciation boundary passed about one thousand miles south of the Atlantic and the Pacific Ocean's modern border. The ocean level dropped by about three hundred feet. Many islands appeared. It could have allowed the *Homo sapiens* to travel from India across the islands to Australia. And some went across the Bering Strait and into the Americas.

Modern archaeological finds continually challenge our understanding of the *Homo sapiens'* migration from Africa. Life was hard for the hunter-gatherers. Conditions were harsh, and disease, hunting accidents, injury, or wild animal attacks could lead to death. The life expectancy of primitive men was short. The world around them was hostile and dangerous. Uncertainty in the world caused them to search for protection and assistance from outside forces. Each clan had its superstitions, worshipped and sacrificed to its idols. The object of worship could be any animal, a carved object, or even nature (such as trees, large stones, mountains, or planets). Today, we know that humanity's history goes back millions of years. Not so long ago, humans proudly declared themselves creatures of God. Stories began of the first man created from the Earth and endowed with an immortal soul. Divine providence created man to be a master over all things on Earth. Everything belongs to humans, the crown of God's creation.

Awareness of their exclusivity filled humanity with pride and delight, a sense of eternal gratitude, and the inexhaustible desire to worship in chants and prayers. But all that came later. In early times, humans had to go through many development stages before becoming masters of the world. First, they had to learn to walk straight, to reach fruits grown on the trees. Then they had to learn to use sticks or stones for hunting. These got them to the top of the food chain. Abilities to defend themselves and attack others. Only then could they push the developing brain to think more efficiently.

TOTEMS AND TABOOS

Like many other animals, primitive people lived in families or clans. Every group had its totem, an object, such as a carved stone, tree, or animal, that reported their ancestry, and they followed the rules made by their ancestors. The totem could be the ancestor of the clan as well as the supreme power. Totems supposedly patronized the members of the clan. Fears and superstitions before the phenomena of nature or predators gave rise to the creation of many primitive pagan totems.

Dr. Sigmund Freud wrote a book called *Totem and Taboo* that outlined the psychoanalytic study of the infantile mental life of primitive man. We can judge the early cave paintings and different myths transferred from generation to generation to understand that they lived in communities (tribes), like much of the rest of the animal world. Still being so close to their animal nature, their instincts pushed them to search for salvation from all the incomprehensible and scary things around them. To make sense of their world, they needed to believe in a force, the power to protect them or maybe even punish and forgive them. The Supreme

Judge is incorruptible and omnipotent. They cherished inherited totems of the tribe clan. Totemism generated numerous taboos regulating almost all aspects of life for this totem's family (group). Taboos were the first codes of conduct for primitive societies.

The word *taboo* itself has several meanings: "holy," "dangerous," "horrifying," "forbidden," and "prohibited."

Belief in totems' protective or punishing power gave rise to pagan beliefs. The tribe leader was the high priest, who ruled his flock using witchcraft, magic and performed various rituals. The leader responds to the group's fears and doubts by creating rites and rituals to explain the unexplainable and maintain order. He orders punishment for violation of taboo or totem rituals. The other members must realize breaking a taboo is punishable by death. The faith in power and protection from the totem had to be unshakable—anyone who doubted could be sacrificed to the totem.

Gullible and obedient cannibals ate their enemies to serve their idols. During totem wars, the victors killed all the men and distributed the captured women among the victors—unless there was a taboo on exogamy, the custom of marrying outside the particular tribe. Wars between different tribes happened when one tribe violated the taboo or insulted the totem of another tribe.

The totem could be either in the middle of a small settlement or somewhere nearby, like on a hill.

Members of the tribe would hold processions with chants and dances, heading to the totem for daily prayer and festivities.

They would make sacrifices in the form of fruits, plants, and even animals, as long as they were not taboo. Sometimes they sacrificed enemies or those who refused to recognize the supremacy of the totem.

The sacrifices were eaten by members of the tribe participating in the festive meal. How were the clans of primitive people organized?

Charles Darwin coined the phrase *"the primal horde"* in his book, *Descent of Man* (1874).

"A form of primitive social organization in which people lived in a small, more or less organized group ruled by an oppressive, authoritarian, and jealous leader (primary father) who appropriated all women and protected them from the encroachment of the sons and the other young men of the tribe. These may have led to a mutiny in which the primary father was killed and eaten."

In *Totem and Taboo*, Freud drew an exact parallel between his clinical observations, finding that all totem religions' quintessence is a ritual consisting of the death of the sacrificial animal, the animal's consumption, and a subsequent mourning period.

In his opinion, Dr. Freud concludes that the first murder is generically (or as a result of evolution) phylogenetically transmitted up to these days and forms a new type of social guilt. To prevent a new murder and the sense of guilt associated with it, the offerings supposedly replaced the father, incest was forbidden, and exogamy was established. Totemism was a practical solution to the "Oedipus complex," a man's primal desire to kill his father and marry his mother.

Totemism preceded the emergence of ethical constraints, religion, and social organization. Freud was fully aware of the hypothetical nature of these constructs. Still, the similarity between his clinical observations and the results of the studies of Darwin, Atkinson, and Robertson-Smith was so striking that he never doubted their fundamental correctness.

Are today's religious rites and restrictions similar to those of totem society? Yes, of course. Most religions' rituals today appealing to any gods use some physical form of worship. Believers often dance, chant, bow, make hand gestures, light candles or sticks, wave cult objects, put hands or objects on bowed heads, and seek protection or forgiveness through prayer.

RELIGION

We believe in multiple signs and actions that protect our homes from evil forces in everyday life. Modern societies have preserved many superstitions and dress code forms of clothing. Some religions cover the heads, and others expose them. Some use amulets and perform various rites daily and during special ceremonies. Today, we gather in prayer houses on certain days of the week. We hold special rites there related to birth, death, or marriage. We strongly believe that without a special ceremony performed by a minister of worship, something could happen for which we have to pay an exorbitant price.

Fear of punishment, doubts, and a strong desire to protect loved ones by adhering to prescribed rituals can justify religious rites. Even the most determined atheist will sometimes accede to certain religious ceremonies.

With the changes in the construction of human communities, there was undoubtedly a change in totemism and religion. Animals have represented gods. We see this in the signs of horns, tails, claws, or other animal symbols on totems.

Religion, though, took the place of a totem symbol. The first public buildings were built for the worship of divinity. Religion became a belief in the omnipotence of the deity, and polytheism became the norm. There were many gods, and faith did not tolerate doubt or disobedience. The tenets of faith had to be strictly enforced.

The next natural step of the civilized community was the transition from polytheism to monotheism, and at this point, an image of a Father God appeared. The worship of God is similar to the genetic memory of the totem worship and joint memorial meal.

The Christian rite of communion followed symbolically eating flesh (wafer) and drinking God's blood (wine). But this is unclear. If God's Son was not guilty, why did He have to be sacrificed? Why is there a Holy Trinity with a Father, Son, and Holy Spirit? What is the original sin of humanity for which Jesus Crist had to die? Maybe human society is guilty of all kinds of sins. But if God is omnipotent and omniscient, doesn't this mean he knew this would happen? So, was it set up, and humanity is still paying, even now?

That is reminiscent of society's totems' part in our ancestors' rituals. Most people feel the need for a defender. We seek one whom we fear but can be trusted. One who has authority but can be imitated, admired, obeyed, loved, and believed. One in whom we can put our hope when we need help.

Creator God has such a persuasive authority. Submission to him in prayers, chants, and rites profoundly influences and transforms. Religion has a more significant impact on people than any form of art or propaganda. Belief in a single God implies the "power of thought." Conviction in the possibility of addressing the Creator with words of prayer, requests, and hopes brings confidence that we can and will be heard.

Throughout the entire period of the existence of our civilization, the difference in religious rites has always been the primary motive for punishing entire countries and nations— in worship rituals, rites, and interpretations.

THE FIRST CIVILIZATIONS

The discovery of grain crops and cereals (wheat, oats, millet, barley, corn, rice) led hunter-gatherers' society to a settled life. People no longer had to travel long distances searching for food but could cultivate the soil and harvest crops stored for a long time. *Homo sapiens* moved on to a sedentary lifestyle and created the first settlements, which led to early civilizations. Some scientists say these lifestyle changes happened because dominant leaders realized the possibility of constructing a steady prayer house instead of temporary structures used in nomadic life. It wasn't a voluntary desire to change hunter-gatherers' free life for the hard work of tillers.

The most ancient civilizations, as we know, are located along the rivers Indus and Ganges in India, on the banks of the Nile in Egypt, the Huanghua and the Yangtze in China.

The Sumerians settled on the fertile lands of southern Mesopotamia between the Tigris and Euphrates rivers at the end of the fourth millennium BC. All these new settlers needed a source of irrigation to cultivate the soil and grow crops.

A settlement dating back twelve millennia was discovered not so long ago in Anatolia, modern-day Turkey. In this settlement, massive, decorated stone pillars were likely religious objects where the colony members gathered for rites and worship. Those people lived in primitive stone homes and also buried their ancestors there.

Although Semite herders inhabited the valley of Mesopotamia, new peoples called Sumerians appeared out of nowhere and were not Semites. The Sumerians sailed on ships and were competent seafarers. They were advanced people with vast knowledge in various fields. Sumerians created the first city-states in Mesopotamia: Erica, Ur, Uruk, Kish, and Lagash.

The Sumerian name became known thanks to a found clay cuneiform with written words: "King Sumer and Akkad." Sumerians called themselves "blackheads." There are many stories about the origins of the Sumerians. One version said they came from somewhere in the southern part of India. Another version claims they came from a place later called the Persian Gulf. The gulf itself was a fertile plateau where people had lived for millennia. However, a catastrophic disaster caused the Indian Ocean's waters to pour in, turning fertile land into the gulf. Perhaps this is how one of the legends of the worldwide flood appeared.

They were responsible for numerous discoveries and inventions: the wheel, cuneiform, mining, smelting of copper and other metals—the use of oil, and the creation of temples and ziggurats for the ancient religions of the world.

The Sumerians, engaged in agriculture, created an extensive irrigation system. They were the first to alloy copper with tin, thus creating bronze and giving rise to the Bronze Age. They were responsible for numerous discoveries and inventions: the wheel, cuneiform, mining, smelting of copper and other metals—the use of oil, and the creation of temples and ziggurats for the ancient religions of the world.

They invented trade and the sexagesimal (a numeral system based on the sixties, which we use even today, (in hours and minutes, for example). They also created a table of zodiac signs and advanced knowledge in astronomy. They knew how to process gold and silver, mine and cut gems. The Sumerians could brew beer, and the Egyptians probably borrowed this knowledge from the Sumerians. Now we know there was intense contact between the Sumerian and Egyptian cultures. The pantheon in Egypt largely coincides with the Sumerian gods.

Astronomical representations of Sumerians and Egyptians are the same. The Sumerians built many different cities. Religion, language, and culture remained common, but each city was an independent state.

The Sumerians worshipped many gods, likely borrowed by Akkad, Babylon, and Assyria. The Akkadian ruler Sargon conquered Sumer in 2361 BC, and under his rule, all of Mesopotamia united under the control of one ruler. Sargon was the first Semitic ruler of Mesopotamia. From 2000 BC, Akkad gradually fell into disrepair and was replaced by Babylon and Assyria.

SUMERIAN SOCIAL SOCIETY

After the Sumerian advances, tribal societies changed to early slave-owning communities. With various valuables (land, property, enslaved people) came classes that united people by societal position and wealth. Nobility and religious ministers owned large pieces of land; many enslaved people worked on these lands. Wealthy merchants owned ships and caravans, which traveled to trade with various countries.

With the advances in society came more power among the religious class too. The high priest's importance increased as people went through him to access God. His power was concentrated and shared with the military ruler. The highest layer of society was occupied by priests who served in the temples. Along with performing religious rites, they also helped build civilization. They were engaged in laying irrigation canals and collecting taxes. They put forward military commanders during periods of military clashes.

The use of cuneiform during the Sumerian reign developed because of trade and taxation. The myth of Gilgamesh, which first mentions the world flood legend, entered numerous nations' epics.

A code of laws regulated shipping issues, relationships, rights, and obligations. This most significant law-and-order reform in ancient Mesopotamia unified the regulations for centuries. It has been reflected in numerous codes across many countries, including biblical legislation. In 1750 BC, Hammurabi, the sixth king of the Amorite First Dynasty of Babylon, had a cuneiform text engraved on a diorite stele, a large stone obelisk.

NEW RELIGION

One seemingly insignificant circumstance occurred around 1800 BC. This event changed the course of history and the development of civilization.

In the Arabian Peninsula and the Middle East, various Semitic tribes led a nomadic life. The Arabs also are the Semites. It is more than likely that some Semitic tribes had developed fertile tracts of land and moved on to a sedentary lifestyle. The way of life changed, and accordingly, new gods appeared. After the gods could not prevent tribe members' deaths, people demanded new rituals, traditions, and a belief in a single all-powerful God. It led to the creation of the Torah, the Pentateuch of Moses. That is included in the first five books in the Judeo-Christian Old Testament.

And God said to Avram (Abraham): "Leave your country. I will give your descendants the land of Canaan."

And Avram built an altar to God, who appeared to him. Avram, a pastoralist dreamer from the Sumerian city of Ur, was visited by a voice from heaven, who commanded him to leave his father's house and go to the country of Canaan. The voice was from the Lord and told that He the Lord and Avram would henceforth be called Abraham. The Lord demanded obedience to Him and the execution of all His orders and promised Abraham that he would have a son one day. Abraham would be the nation's patriarch innumerable "as the sand of the sea" (Gen. 32:12).

Abraham married the beautiful Sarah (his half-sister) and later, to his great sadness, found that she could not have children. She lamented because she could not produce an heir to inherit their possessions. Sarah could not fulfill Abraham's dream of an heir. He believed in this monotheistic deity, settled in Canaan, and pitched his tents near Mamre (Hebron). His wishes for an heir still did not happen. Sarah wanted to please Abraham, and as a tradition of the times dictated, she brought her servant, Agar, to him. Abraham was with Agar, and she bore him a boy named Ishmael. He became known as the Arabs' father, and even the lineage of Muhammad is traced back to him.

Finally, the Lord decided to fulfill the oath, and Sarah gave birth to a boy named Isaac. Because Sarah was jealous of Agar, she and the infant had to leave.

Isaac accepted his father's beliefs in the single God and became the second biblical patriarch.

Years later, Isaac married and had two sons, Esau and Jacob. God blessed his younger son, Jacob, and gave him another name: Israel. The Torah describes Israel's Jacob story; he went to his mother's homeland for his bride. There he worked for his uncle, Laban.

Jacob spent fourteen years working hard to get married to Laban's two daughters.

He became the father of twelve sons and the ancestor of Israel's twelve tribes (families). They adopted Jacob's religion of ancestors, monotheism.

The Torah narrates Jacob/Israel's history and how his whole family (Hebrews) ended up in Egypt and enslaved for many years: some say 425 years and some only 210 years. Some sources even claim that the Egyptian bondage of the Hebrews is just a myth.

At the end of the slavery period, the Torah tells how this single God sent the prophet Moses to rescue the Hebrews (Jews) from Egypt, called the exodus. The Jews were miraculously saved when Moses parted the Red Sea. They had to wander through the desert for forty years, and Moses received the Ten Commandments from God on Mount Sinai.

From this moment, the countdown of the Jews as a nation begins. Unfortunately, the only known source for the exodus is the Torah itself. According to one hypothesis, Abraham's era began in the twentieth century BC, based on calculating the exodus from Egypt to Solomon's temple's construction was about 480 years.

Another hypothesis, which Dr. Sigmund Freud shared in his book *Man Moses: The Psychology of Religion*, questions the timeline and Moses's existence. Freud believed the Egyptian pharaoh Amenhotep introduced monotheism when he became the supreme priest to Aton, the Sun God. Amenhotep built a new capital and named it Akhet-Aton. He changed his name to Akhenaton (Echnaton) and married his beautiful cousin Nefertiti. The priests were not powerful enough to hold the pharaoh accountable for deviating from ancient traditions. In the seventeenth year of his rule, Akhenaton was overthrown. One of his sons, Tutankhamun, moved the capital back to Thebes. Priests persecuted followers of the new religion of the deposed pharaoh. Priests did order to erase Akhenaton's name from all monuments.

Moses (or Moshe in Hebrew) is the Egyptian word for "mose- child." Legend tells how he was rescued as a baby from a wicker basket floating on the Nile River. Such legends about miraculous salvation were quite common when it came to royalty. Such legends were of King Sargon of Akkad and similar legends of Cyrus, Romulus, Hercules, Oedipus, and others.

It would make sense if Moses were an Egyptian. The tradition of circumcision was more likely adopted in Egypt. Not in any other country in Mesopotamia or the Mediterranean did such a custom exist.

The Torah interprets the tradition of circumcision as a sign of the union between God and Abraham. It tells us how God was angry with Moses for neglecting the sacred custom regarding his son. God wanted to kill Moses, but his wife, originally from the land of Midian, saved him by hastily organizing circumcision for Moses's son.

Dr. Freud suggests that Moses may have been a nobleman who may have been a member of the royal

Akhenaton family. Still, perhaps with the pharaoh's death, Moses's ambitious hopes of inheriting the throne and establishing a new religion collapsed. Unwilling to renounce his beliefs, he decided to create a new state with a new people and religion.

In another version, about two hundred years before Akhenaten's rule, the Semitic Gixoso tribes seized power in northern Egypt. Moses could choose them as his future people. The exodus from Egypt in 1350 BC was peaceful, according to Freud. There were no protected borders. It happened after Akhenaton's death. Historians believe that the Jewish tribes, from which the people of Israel later emerged, adopted a new religion. But it happened not in the Sinai Peninsula but Meribel-Kades in modern-day Arabia. The Arab tribes of Median, the God Yahweh's worshippers, lived there, an oasis rich in springs. Yahweh was believed to be the God of volcanoes. One of the mountains along the western border of Arabia may have been called Sinai-Horiw. Moses was the son-in-law of the Median priest Jofor, possibly the ancestor of the priests of Cades, adopting a common belief for all, the worship of the God Yahweh.

The Pentateuch of Moses and Joshua Navin's book are first mentioned by one of the priests, a contemporary of King David. After the decline of the Northern Kingdom of Israel, Jewish priests united both parts.

The essential component of the religion of Judaism was Mashiach's parish (Hebrew) or Messiah's belief.

The Messiah had to come from the House of David and establish fairness, honesty, abundance, and peace. The dead would resurrect, and universal prosperity would come.

Any religion is based on a belief in the afterlife. Hope for justice in the afterlife and fear of eternal punishment for sins before the Lord make people obedient. The ability to repent and receive absolution makes religion even more attractive.

Returning to the Torah, we learn that sometime around 1,000 BC, a young shepherd named David defeated the giant Goliath and became the Jewish people's king. He won the battle for a small village called Jerusalem and established it as the new country's capital. Modern archaeological excavations confirm the existence of the House of David. Solomon, son of David, about whom many legends exist, built a temple to honor God. Solomon's temple stood for five years after Solomon's death (975 or 930 BC). Solomon's son Rehoboam could not hold the country together. Ten northern tribes broke away and created the state of Israel, with the capital in Samaria. Two southern tribes created the land of Judea, with the capital in Jerusalem.

Egyptian pharaoh Shoshenq (Shishak I) attacked the Jewish state and plundered the First Temple in the tenth century BC.

Samaria still was the capital of Israel's northern state. In 732–722 BC, the Assyrian king Sargon II captured northern Israel's capital, took captive all the ten tribes, and scattered them among other nations. Other people from the conquered lands settled these territories. Later they were called Samaritans.

In 605 BC, the Babylonian king Nebuchadnezzar besieged Jerusalem and took noble families hostage. The Temple was burned and destroyed. Nebuchadnezzar also ruined the city walls. Nebuchadnezzar returned in 586 BC to plunder all the First Temple treasures and took away most of the population.

PERSIANS

The Persians were one of the Iranian-speaking (Farsi) tribes that came to Mesopotamia. In 539 BC, the Persians, led by Cyrus the Great, captured Babylonia, turning it into an Achaemenid Empire colony. Cyrus the Great, the king of Persia, decided to restore law and order. He allowed many captured nations to return to their homelands.

Ezra was a priest and religious leader among captured Jews who led to return from Babylon to Jerusalem. In the book of Ezra, the Jews of Babylon were allowed to return and rebuild the Temple of God. The Jewish priest Ezra and Nehemiah, who was taken into Babylonian captivity and returned to Judea, restored the Temple of Jerusalem around 500 BC. The consolidation of the Jews occurred nine hundred years after the appearance of Moses. According to biblical science, the book of Ezra-Nehemiah has been called the Restoration book after codifying the Pentateuch for the Jewish people.

Ezra demanded that all Jews who had pagans families must send them back with their shared children. The dissenters who kept pagan wives had to go with them.

This coup paved the way for isolationism, extreme fanaticism, and obstacles to conversion to Judaism.

Such ultra-orthodox religion lasted millennia, suffering from many wars and destruction attempts. It has survived, and the Jews returned to their ancestors' land in the twentieth century. The same religion caused persecution and torment. Excommunicating Jews from their faith could disperse them from other nations. Perhaps the bitter cup of torture and suffering would have passed by, but the nation could be dispersed and disappear from the face of the Earth, like many other nations. This biblical history of the Torah formed the basis of the three major religions of the human race and defined civilization's ways for millennia. By accepting faith in a single God, humanity created and destroyed in the name of God, crashing anything that might ruin or hinder faith in the omnipotence of the chosen deity.

Preaching national exclusivity, Ezra laid a time bomb that repeatedly put the Jews on the brink of survival.

MONOTHEISM

The three main Abrahamic religions of the world—Judaism, Christianity, and Islam—have been at odds with each other for the right to be the only and true religion for all humankind for centuries. Judaism is based on the Abrahamic monotheistic religion.

Christianity appeared as one of the many sects in Judaism, which disagreed with the primary doctrine of the ruling faith, quickly moved away from Judaism, and proclaimed a new God-son, Jesus Christ.

Christians saw the birth of Jesus Christ as a starting point in the calendar. The estimated date of the birth of Jesus Crist established the concept of the new era. Recorded events around the life and death of Jesus (Evangelie) forming the new religion are known as the New Testament, the writings of the four apostles of Jesus Christ.

Islam, or the Muslim faith, was established in Western Arabia at the beginning of the seventh century. Like Judaism and Christianity, Islam is based on the Abrahamic religion, monotheism.

Alexander the Great (356 BC–323 BC) conquered the Persian Empire, and after his death, his descendants/

commanders divided the conquered territories. As part of this heritage, the Seleucid dynasties took control of Asia Minor, the Middle East, and Judea, and the Ptolemies took over Egypt.

These were heirs/military leaders of Alexander the Great (Diadochi in Greek), Ptolemies in Egypt, and Seleucids in Asia who waged constant wars for influence in the Middle East. Attacked continuously from one side or the other, Judea was in the middle of those interests (trade routes from India, the Far East, and Egypt, by the Mediterranean Sea to Europe).

Rome, the new player for world domination, conquered both Egypt and Syrian possessions. Judea became a vassal of Rome. The population of the country constantly rebelled, seeking to restore independence. Emperor Hadrian resolutely put things in order "in the Roman way." The country's population was expelled without the right to reside on the country's territory, the capital Jerusalem was renamed Aelia Capitalina, and Judea was given a new name, Palestine.

It was renamed after Syria Palestine, a province of the Roman Empire, by the Roman emperor Hadrian in 135 AD. to erase the memory of the Kingdom of Judah. "Palaestina" (the Latin version of the Greek name for Palestine) comes from "Philistia," the name of the part of the Mediterranean coast of modern Israel inhabited in ancient times by the Philistines.

The Christian movement began to accept non-Jewish members. It moved from strict rules imposed on

Jews. It gradually became a new and separate religion. Emperor Nero blamed the Christians for the Great Fire of Rome in 64 AD. All Christians in Rome were arrested, tortured, and killed. But with time sect grew as a Christian church, and in 313 AD, Emperor Constantine issued the Edict of Milan, which accepted Christianity.

THE MACCABEES REBELLION

(167–160 BCE)

Jewish rebellions against the Seleucids are associated with the oppression of religion and the planting of Greek culture and religion. After numerous battles, the Jewish army expelled the Seleucid troops, and the Hasmonean dynasty reigned in the country.

Judea needed support to fight Syria and allied with Rome. In 63 BC, the Roman legions under Pompey the Great's command entered Judea. The country turned from an ally into a vassal.

After Judea's conquest, Pompey executed the rebel leaders and imposed high taxes on Judea and Jerusalem. Judea rebelled many times against the invaders. Gabiny, the Roman commander, suppressed the revolt of the Jews in 55 BC. He had to conquer many fortresses that resisted fiercely. In these battles, young Mark Antony stood out.

In the same year, Marcus Licinius Crassus, a Roman general and politician who helped turn Rome from a republic into an empire, replaced Avl Gabiny.

He also robbed the Temple of Jerusalem, taking two thousand talents of gold (about one hundred fifty thousand pounds). Crassus died in the campaign against Parthia. A small detachment led by Guy Cassius Longin was able to make its way back to Syria. The Jews rebelled again, but Cassius was able to suppress it.

Julius Caesar sent two legions to Syria in 49 BC to subjugate Judea and fight his opponent, Pompey the Great. During the war with Pompey, Caesar went to Egypt, seeking help from the Jews, who hated Pompey. Caesar won, and Pompey was killed. Caesar restored Cleopatra's power and proclaimed her queen. The people of Alexandria and the Egyptian army rebelled against Caesar, but he got help from the Mithridates of Pergamon and Judea's rulers to suppress the rebellion. With Caesar came the rise of the Roman Empire.

Herod the Great ruled around the time of the second Caesar. He was not a Jew by birth but practiced some form of Judaism. Under his rule, there was constant unrest in Judea.

In Rome, these problems in Judea provoked adverse reactions.

The second Roman Caesar, Octavian Augustus, who beat Mark Antony in the power struggle, forgave Mark Antony's faithful friend, Herod, and even approved him to be Judea's king.

Under the Roman Caesar, Tiberius, the procurator of Judea, Pontius Pilate, condemned Jesus Christ to be crucified.

The fourth Roman emperor, Caligula, was inadequate. He demanded that his people honor him as a god on Earth, and he demanded that his statue be placed in all religious temples. Judea was preparing to rebel, but guards killed Caligula in a conspiracy.

The fifth Roman Emperor, Claudius, Caligula's uncle, was poisoned with mushrooms by his wife and niece Agrippina (Nero's mother).

The sixth Roman Caesar was Nero. He murdered his mother and was a cruel tyrant who persecuted the Christians.

Herod the Great ruled around the time of the second Caesar. He was not a Jew by birth but practiced some form of Judaism. People did not like Herod. He was cruel and devoted to Rome. Under his rule, there was constant unrest in Judea.

In Rome, problems in Judea provoked adverse reactions.

Nero sent Vespasian, the founder of the Flavian dynasty, to suppress the uprising in Judea.

CHRISTIANITY

During the Roman period of domination in Judea, oppressions united many different religious groups connected at the spiritual-mystical level in interpreting the Torah.

The Pharisees, a Jewish religious party, considered themselves chosen and were the most respected and numerous groups. They were a monastic brotherhood. The Sadducees denied the resurection, accepting wrriten Law. They kept themselves apart. The Essenes, a Jewish ascetic groups were considered a different brotherhood from the Qumran community. They considered themselves a purely messianic brotherhood, more like a monastic order.

In Judea, there was constant unrest and uprisings. Different from all other fraternities stood a religious group called the Zealots of faith or just Zealots. They were convinced there would be a holy war with the occupiers, the Roman authorities. They felt that war was the only way to bring the Messiah.

In this political situation, baby Jesus was born by the Virgin Mary. (It was such a profound event that in AD 500, the monk Dionysius Exiguus, on behalf of Pope

John I, prepared a new chronology to make the birth of Jesus Christ the starting point for the calendar.) At this time, Judea was ruled by Rome, by the heirs of Herod the Great. His son, Herod Antipas, took possession of Galilee and Perea (an area on the Jordan River). Herod Antipas ruled from AD 4–49. He was the king who ordered John the Baptist's arrest and execution. To Herod Antipas, the Roman governor Pontius Pilate sent arrested Jesus, a native of Galilee, who was under Herod Antipas's jurisdiction. Herod Antipas sent him back to Pontius Pilate.

By this time, Jesus Christ was thirty-three years old. What was he doing, and what did people know about him then?

One of the first historians who mentions Christ is the famous Flavius Josephus (AD 38–100). Josephus (born Yosef ben Mattiahu) was a Pharisee and a deeply religious Jew. Josephus was born into a religious family of Maccabees and high priests. There is much evidence in Christian literature for the life and writings of Josephus. In one of his works, he wrote:

At that time was a wise man called Jesus. His lifestyle was commendable, and he was famous for his virtue; many Jews and others became his followers. Pilatus condemned him to crucifixion, and he died, but those who became his followers did not deny his doctrine. They said he appeared to them on the third day after his crucifixion and was alive. That means he is the Messiah, of which the prophets foreshadowed miracles. Many people among the Jews and other peoples became his adepts." (J. Flavius – *The Jewish Wars*).

Many biblical scholars did not doubt this text was a late insertion. We don't know whether Jesus was a historical figure or a mystical character with many followers who were eventually called Christian believers. It was a troubled time in Judea, and many preachers and prophets of various kinds roamed the country, prophesying the coming of the Messiah and the world's end. Thus, Christianity was born.

Saul of Tarsus (3–67) was a Pharisee who received an excellent education in the religious school known as the rabbinical academy. He did not meet Jesus personally, but on the way to Damascus, Saul did receive a vision and became a devoted follower of Christ. Saul became the apostle Paul, a teacher, organizer, and church founder. He systematized Christian teachings and preached the final separation from Judaism. Apostle Paul fervently rebelled against the need for the gentiles who became Christians to keep the law of Moses (circumcision).

Some believe that Nero ordered Paul to be put to a martyr's death.

The life of Jesus was recorded in four writings, which began in the New Testament and appeared in AD 64–69. The first is Matthew's Gospel, written by Matthew, the son of Alphaeus, a tax collector for the Roman Empire and a follower of Jesus Christ. The Gospel of Mark consists of a description of Jesus's life, sermons, and miracles. Some researchers believe that the text more likely belongs to a Christian Jew. The Gospel of Luke begins with the prediction of the birth of John the Baptist. Like all the other gospels, it was translated into Greek. The Gospel of John shows that Jesus Christ is the Son of God. It focuses on his miracles, entrance to Jerusalem, the Last Supper, crucifixion, burial, and resurrection. The crux of all the gospels and Christianity is that Christ was raised from the dead after the crucifixion because the resurrection proves he is the Son of God and Messiah. Many people doubt the resurrection took place. Some say the body was stolen. The Christians say that Christ appeared to his apostles and walked among them, teaching them till he was taken back to heaven.

The basic tenet of all gospels is that Christ was resurrected after the crucifixion. On this tenet, the Christian religion is based. Because Christ was resurrected, He is the Son of God and the Messiah. Unfortunately, His miracle resurrection was not seen by anyone. Someone said that two women who came to the place saw His silhouette, fled in fear, and did not say anything to anyone. We know from evangelists that Christ appeared to His apostles alive until He was taken to heaven.

In the Jewish religion, old prophecies predicted a savior, a Messiah (*Mashiach* in Hebrew), from the House of David. He would arrive in Jerusalem riding on a female donkey. He would establish peace on Earth.

Joshua (Jesus) was a stray preacher accused of blasphemy for proclaiming himself Messiah and then executed by the Roman authorities. His name would have remained unknown, as were the names of many other itinerant preachers, but resurrection made Him God.

But as the legend goes, the Roman ruler Titus Flavius, the conqueror of Judea, enlisted Joseph Flavius to create an alternative Jewish religion. According to Titus Flavius, these people willing to die for their religion could only be defeated by giving them new faith and a new God. Titus saw that the Jewish priests sacrificed their God even after the Roman warriors broke into the temple and killed many people, and blood was pouring everywhere. By creating the right religion, Titus reasoned, we can manage people without wars and will no longer need soldiers to guard the borders. And Rome had thousands of miles of borders to defend.

Perhaps the new religion was initially started to control the always-rebellious Judea. Josephus was an ideal figure for creating such faith. He was born into a family of Jewish priests and knew the Greek language well. He spent three years in the desert as an ascetic hermit who passed through the three main sects of the time: the Pharisees, the Sadducees, and the Essenes. Josephus said his decision to surrender to Vespasian, the Roman emperor who founded the Flavian Dynasty, came with a revelation from above. The task of encouraging belief in a new God and a different religion could only be on the shoulders of an extraordinary person, a connoisseur of the Torah. But even for him alone, such a gigantic task was impossible. Many people probably worked to create the right religion for ruling Rome.

There had been many Jewish sects long before the official recognition of Christianity. Sects of the Eastern Persian cult of the god Mithras, for example. This cult was widespread in the countries of Central Asia. There were a lot of similar rites between the cult of Mithras and Christianity.

In 1947, some scrolls were found written long before Christ's appearance in areas of the Dead Sea of Qumran. They tell about the existence of the Essene sect and its teaching. The manuscripts are remarkably similar to the writings of "sacred scripture" written by Greek evangelists. The scrolls talked about the Messiah, the Son of God, who could be accepted if all of the Torah's prophecies followed. The Torah is filled with predictions associated with the coming of the Messiah.

Creating a new religion required not a militant Messiah but a call for goodness, love, and humility. Jesus Christ preached to love your enemy and give Caesar what was Caesar's.

He was perfect for a Roman god. He needed to be raised from the dead to be seen as God. Of course, the first Christians were Jews and Jesus with his apostles. One thing that made Christianity attractive to new converts was that men didn't need to be circumcised. Instead, new believers were baptized with water.

So, why would Josephus help the Romans? Even from his books, it is known that he participated in the uprising against the Romans in AD 66–74. During the siege of Jerusalem, Joseph appealed to the fortress's Jewish defenders to surrender to the Romans. After the defeat, he was arrested by the Romans and appeared before the commander, Vespasian Flavius. Josephus predicted Vespasian Flavius would become the Roman Caesar. When Vespasian became the first Caesar of the Flavius Dynasty, Joseph, who received the surname Flavius, became a Roman citizen, settled in one of the Flavius estates, and wrote his famous works *Jewish Wars, Jewish Antiquities,* and *Objection to Apian.* During the siege of Jerusalem, Joseph appealed to the fortress's Jewish defenders to surrender to the Romans.

The Roman army destroyed Jerusalem in AD 70. Rome gave Titus and Vespasian a grand triumphal parade. Under the triumphal arch of Titus passed the defeated prisoners, carrying numerous captured trophies.

Judea continued to rebel against Roman domination. The uprising in AD 115–117 was the Second Jewish War. The rebellion swept through Mesopotamia, Egypt, Cyprus, and Palestine.

Under Emperor Trajan's command, the Roman army fought against the Parthian Empire. Trajan dispatched General Lucius Quietus, appointing him governor of Judea. When Rome got a new emperor, Hadrian, he recalled and executed Lucius Quietus.

The third uprising occurred under the leadership of Bar Kokhba in AD 132-136. At first, it was successful, and Bar Kokhba was proclaimed the Messiah. But then, Emperor Hadrian summoned the commander Julius Severus from Britain. After three years of struggle in AD 136 and six Roman legions, the uprising was suppressed, and Bar Kokhba was killed.

Hadrian turned Jerusalem into a pagan city, banning the Jewish people from living there. Under the penalty of death, he forbade the Jewish faith. Hadrian renamed Judea to Palestine so that the word *Judea* would disappear forever. Jerusalem was named Aelia Capitolina. He issued a decree in which the Jewish people had no right to step on the city's territory. The Jews were in exile for two thousand years.

As we know, the first Christians were Jewish. Proselytism in Judaism never was welcome. It was a closed sect. In contrast, Christianity was open to anyone who wished to believe. The proselytes (the new adherents) were required to undergo baptism instead of bloody and painful circumcision.

Constantine, the Great—Roman emperor (AD 306-337)— converted to Christianity, affirming Rome's dominant religion. Rafael's painting *Baptism of Constantine* shows the emperor kneeling before the bishop, who performs the rite of baptism.

Emperor Constantine convened the First Council of Nice in AD 325. It was the Christian bishop's first council (ecumenical) held in the Bithynian city (now Turkey) of Nicaea. Having proclaimed a final separation from Judaism, they declared Sunday as a day off instead of Saturday. They adopted canons about the Easter celebration to make this day different from the Judean Pesach (Passover).

Aurelius Augustine, better known as Blessed Augustine (354–430), was one of the Christian Church fathers and Christian philosophy creator. In his *Faust's Answer to Manichaeism*, Augustine wrote: *"Jews are guilty of the blood of Christ ... cursed from the Earth ... damned by the Church. Preserve the testimonies for Christian believers in what enslavement of those who, in the pride of their domination, has sentenced the Lord to death ... marked with Cain's seal."*

Pope Innocent III (1198–1216) denounced Jewish abuses. He complained that Jews were "charging an excessive rate of interest; they had built a synagogue in Sens that was taller than the neighboring church; they appeared in public on Good Friday and jeered at Christians; and they were receivers of stolen goods and murderers of Christians."

In response, Innocent III issued a series of four anti-Jewish canons promulgated at the Fourth Lateran Council (1215). He banned excessive interest rates and forbade Jews from appearing publicly during Holy Week and holding public office. He also required them to wear distinctive clothing (a practice continued under Hitler's regime).

Martin Luther (1483–1546) was a Catholic priest who translated the Bible into German against the Church's wishes. He initiated the Protestant Reformation by posting his ninety-five theses on the Wittenberg church door. When the Jews refused to accept his message of salvation, he responded with a treatise called *Jews and Lies*, in which he wrote:

1. Jewish synagogues should be burned
2. Jewish homes to be destroyed
3. Jews should be given the work of servants and lackeys
4. Jewish money should be confiscated
5. Jews should be expelled by force from their communities

Jules Isaac, author of *Has Anti-Semitism Roots in Christianity*, wrote, "Christian anti-Semitism is a powerful stem with strong roots from which (in the Christian world) all other types of anti-Semitism grow, even those that are anti-Christian in nature."

ISLAM

Islam started in the early seventh century in Western Arabia. The founder of Islam was the Prophet Muhammad (571–632). In his sermons, the Prophet Muhammad claims he purified the true faith in the One God from the distortions made by Jews, Christians, and Gentiles. Muhammad was a cruel person, which was one of the reasons for the success of Islam. Cruelty is one of many qualities that people inherited from their ancestors. Islam has always been active in proselytism.

Islam has always been a religion of aggression and, many times, forced proselytism. To be converted, one must utter the Shahada, or the prayer of faith, that says: "I testify that there is no other God but Allah, and I prove that Muhammad is Allah's messenger." This oath should be done in front of witnesses as a symbol of faith. Circumcision of adult proselytes was considered optional.

There is no clear line in Islam that separates religion and law. Islamic nations are governed by Sharia law (a set of Muslim religious, legal, and domestic rules based on the Koran).

One of the pillars of Islam is spiritual jihad (fighting for faith).

Islamization is the conversion of entire populations captured during the Arab conquest.

After the Prophet Muhammad died in 632, his followers on the Arabian Peninsula established an Arab Caliphate. The United Arab tribes moved to conquer the world. Iraq, Syria, Egypt, the Persian Empire, North Africa, Byzantium, Mesopotamia, and Palestine came under the Caliphate's control.

The conquests of Islam spread to the Middle East, Southeast Asia, and Africa. In 711, the Arabs invaded the Iberian Peninsula and moved on to Europe. In 732, they were defeated in the Battle of Tours at Poitiers, which halted Islam's advance.

In 1923, the Treaty of Lausanne settled the conflict between the Ottoman Empire and the Allies of World War I. Turkey gave up claims to the Ottoman Empire, and the Allies recognized the Republic of Turkey as a sovereign nation.

RELIGION AND CIVILIZATION

Humanity has seen numerous religions over the millennia, and the idea of worship is a vital part of civilization. The central role of religion, with its symbolic rites, is to worship something, whether it's an image or a being. And faith acted as a carrier of philosophy, art, history, and custodian of covenants of past generations for transmission to descendants.

Any religion based on a belief in extraordinary supernatural power could be decisive, capable of influencing human souls at birthdays and continuing after physical life. It gave people meaning in their daily existence. It also gave a spiritual blessing, a belief in the soul's immortality. This belief in an afterlife gave adherents hope and faith in a bright, serene existence. One had to believe and observe the traditional rites and sacrifices to God through the cult's ministers.

The factions' servants became wealthy owners of valuable goods, property, and lands. Religious authorities sanctifying and supporting secular power could affect the authorities' very existence if they came into conflict with the clergy. Religious leadership, as they controlled people's minds, could influence even the kings.

Religion was a potent political force with almost limitless power. When Christianity took hold in Europe and the Middle East, intolerance of other faiths or apostasy from canons and religious dogmas were punished mercilessly and publicly to discourage other rebels.

Christianity created the Inquisition, organized the Crusades, burned "witches" on fires, and destroyed and persecuted all who dared to doubt the Christian God's powers and worshiped false gods.

The conquests of Islam spread to the Middle East, Southeast Asia, and Africa. In 711, the Arabs invaded the Iberian Peninsula and moved on to Europe. In 732, they were defeated in the Battle of Tours at Poitiers, which halted Islam's advance.

Al-Andalus—Muslim Spain (711–1492)—was taken back by the Catholic king's troops after almost eight centuries of occupancy. In 1299, the Osmans' Turkic tribes, the Islamic Ottoman Empire, captured Constantinople, renaming it Istanbul.

In 1923, the Treaty of Lausanne settled the conflict between the Ottoman Empire and the Allies of World War I. Turkey gave up claims to the Ottoman Empire, and the Allies recognized the Republic of Turkey as a sovereign nation.

THE RIGHTS OF THE STRONGEST

The conquest by Alexander the Great (356–323 BC) of the Persian Empire marked a new reality in interstate relations. Even significantly outnumbered, a strong and determined commander can conquer other countries. Massive wealth accumulated can be captured by winning a war. The winner gets everything. The loser becomes a tributary state. It's believed that Alexander the Great, acquainted with the Persian religion of Mithra, was thinking about creating a new religion, combining Mithraism with Greek. His early death prevented these plans.

The Roman Empire had created a powerful, disciplined army and moved to conquer all the territories under the Diadochs (Latin for *generals*) of Alexander the Great. Rome led constant wars, seeking to subdue the barbarians and make them the tributaries of Rome.

The Roman Empire was finally divided into Western and Eastern empires in 476. The Western Roman Empire fell and formally dissolved its imperial court in 480. The Eastern Roman Empire, centered in Constantinople, existed for almost another thousand years until 1452.

During a Roman civil war, Constantine I defeated Licinius in 324 at the Battle of Adrianopolis. This victory made the Christian Church a more potent assistant to the monarch. Due to partition in 395, the Eastern Roman Empire declared itself a Byzantine Empire with a Christian Orthodox religious center in Constantinople. The Byzantine Empire's pagan neighbors—Moravia, Bulgaria, and later Kyiv, were baptized in 988. Most territories were inherited by Russia and celebrated by the Russian Church as the beginning of Christianity in Russia.

In the West, Frankish King Charles the Great (or Charlemagne) was crowned by the Roman bishop of Leo III. In 962, Pope John XII proclaimed the Great Otto I emperor of the Holy Roman Empire.

In Europe, Christianity was established with Catholic Rome under the leadership of the pope as its center.

The Norman Conquest of England (eleventh through fourteenth centuries) in the Middle Ages by Duke William the Conqueror marked England's Christianization. Sweden, Norway, and Denmark adopted the Christian faith during the same period. Christians organized the Crusades to retake Palestine, which Muslims had occupied. Kings, peasants, soldiers, and clergypersons all went to fight for the Holy Sepulcher's liberation from the infidels. The Crusades had a powerful impact on all sectors of society. Ideas of crusaders' hikes began in the late eleventh century and blossomed in the twelfth century.

THE LATER MIDDLE AGES

(Thirteenth-Fifteenth Centuries)

Muslim countries united by the Ottoman Empire prevented European nations from trading with the East, so they sought alternative routes to India and the Far East. For the Christian missionaries, this meant unprecedented opportunities to convert millions of pagans to the "right" faith. It led to the discovery of the American continent by Christopher Columbus.

During his life, Genghis Khan began a campaign to conquer Central Asia. He destroyed the cities of Khujand, Bukhara, Samarkand, and many other fortresses. In the Far East, the Mongols' countless hordes, united under Genghis Khan's leadership, poured west. Mongols treated the populations in this region with brutal violence, and survivors were captured.

After the campaign to Eastern Iran, the Mongols began to conquer the Caucasian states. The time came for Crimea. There was a battle on the Kalka River in modern-day Ukraine between the Russian tribes and the Mongol army. After a long struggle, the Mongols were victorious and slaughtered the Russians before returning to Genghis Khan.

The Mongols successfully conquered the territories of Anatolia and moved to the Middle East. In Palestine, the Mongols captured Samaria and Gaza. Baghdad and Syria expressed obedience to the conquerors.

The army of Egyptian Mamluks was able to defeat the Mongols.

Descendants of Genghis Khan had assembled a vast hundred twenty thousand to one hundred fifty thousand people army and moved to conquer Eastern and Central Europe. As a part of the Mongolian Empire, Bashkiria and Volga Bulgaria were captured and included in the Golden Horde, conquered lands the Mongols settled. Khan Batu, Genghis's grandson, led the campaign to Russia. The captured cities included: Ryazan, Kolomna (after a long resistance), Moscow, Vladimir, Pereslavl-Zalessky, Tver, Torzhok, and Kozelsk. The Mongols decided not to go to Novgorod but returned to the Eurasian steppe for rest and fattened their horses.

The Golden Horde raided Russia in the following years, even in the siege and capturing Kyiv in 1214. The Mongols also attacked Poland, Hungary, Croatia, Serbia, and Bulgaria.

The ancient religion of the Mongols was shamanism, and a large part of their population was a nonbeliever.

The Golden Horde was a Turkic state. The conquest of the Turks facilitated the eventual formation of the Ottoman Empire.

Most of today's Turks are Muslims, but some Orthodox Christians and Buddhists have also become Muslims.

Today in Russia, there is a new theory denying the Mongolian yoke's existence in Russia and the invasion or conquest by Tatar-Mongols of European territories. It is considered an attempt to hide the real reasons for strife and civil wars: greed for power.

Now let us look at the United States of America.

DISCOVERY OF AMERICA

Hoping to open trade routes to India, Christopher Columbus discovered in 1492 a new continent later named America. After asking for help for years, Aragon's Catholic monarchs agreed to sponsor his journey.

The tremendous geographical discovery marked the beginning of a new era: colonialism. The Spanish crown rightfully declared the open lands its colony. Spain's colonization brought Catholicism and the Spanish language to most of the new countries in South America. The wealth flowing into the Spanish treasury led the way to the rest of the world. Suddenly, monarchs all over claimed the right to exploit human and natural resources and monopolize world trade with new and unique methods. Gaining disenfranchised labor, exploiting natural resources, and aboriginal labor as enslaved people made Spain and her colonies incredibly rich.

Africa became the primary supplier of enslaved people to work on overseas plantations. Enslaved people were captured in battles or bought from local princes, shackled, transported across the ocean, and sold on slave markets.

Britain became the most significant colonial power, subduing Australia, India, and Hong Kong and leading the Opium Wars against China. France subjugated Algeria, Vietnam, Cambodia, and Laos. Portugal subjugated Brazil and many islands.

Russia was engaged in successful conquests of Siberia, Kavkaz, and Central Asia. There was a real war for territories in North America among Spain, England, France, the Netherlands, and Sweden. Russia also got in on the act and subjugated Alaska.

The discovery of America was a new milestone in the history of humankind. It changed the world forever. All colonial territories received the language and faith of the colonizers. The ongoing development of new territories required a robust expansion of shipbuilding. The influx of significant silver and gold volumes contributed to radical changes in world trade and the rapid growth of science and technology: new products and goods revitalized business and agricultural production.

With a vast new land came new ideas for creating a society. Significant shifts in the public consciousness—a new structure of society. What was the reason for people going to America?

In America, the first English colony was the Plymouth Colony, and its first settlers were passengers of the famous *Mayflower*. They were Puritans (English Protestants).

In 1532, the Reformation came to Britain. The initiator of the Reformation in England was King Henry

VIII, whom the pope forbade from divorcing Catherine of Aragon.

Then the Synod of Bishops of England declared the Anglican Church independent of the Vatican.

King James I advised the Puritans to recognize the supremacy of the Anglican Church or leave England. Many Puritans decided to build their futures in the New World. Thousands of their fellow believers followed the first Puritans to leave for America. They were not criminals but, on the contrary, decent citizens. They founded a colony—Massachusetts, centered in the village of Boston. Massachusetts has become a haven for the persecuted Puritans in their homeland.

Next on the map of the American continent appeared Maryland. Like the rest of the settlements, it was inhabited by people strong in their faith who wanted to build a new society. The main virtue considered would be religious tolerance, in which they would be free from oppression and persecution.

Pennsylvania became a colony of religious minorities. The Quakers were persecuted in England. They came to America and laid a new city—Philadelphia. Representatives of other denominations persecuted in their homeland also left for America: Huguenots, Mennonites, Methodists, and Baptists.

Of course, most people left for the United States for financial reasons. And there were quite a few of them. The state of Georgia was founded by poor people who were released from prisons for debts they could not pay.

King George II established a settlement in America for prisoners. In January 1733, a ship with 120 colonists on board docked in Charleston.

People immigrated to America during Ireland's Great Famine, which lasted from 1846 to 1851. One and a half million people left Ireland.

Many people were attracted by the opportunity of education in America. In 1636, Boston had the first university in America—Harvard College. By the beginning of the War of Independence, there were already nine colleges in America.

Very educated people also went to America. Undoubtedly among the new settlers were crooks, con artists, and beggars. Most of the population wished for freedoms (religion, race, social and other inequalities). However, the foremost opportunity was to apply their strength and skills to build a new, free life for themselves and their descendants.

People suddenly thought of a free, equal, and independent existence. America declared independence from its colonizer, Britain, in 1776 and fought the Revolutionary War against Britain to win its freedom.

Proclaimed rights and liberties had a profound impact on practically all of humanity. The new American society created the United States' fundamental law, the US Constitution (ratified in 1788), and declared justice, life, freedom, and property rights for all.

The Founding Fathers created a profound and unique document in the Constitution that ensured a checks-and-balances system that gives power to the people through the states.

The Constitution of the United States, created by the Founding Fathers, has shown the strength of government institutions and the law's supremacy for almost a quarter of a millennium.

Among the new immigrants were adventurers of a different kind. Free enterprise is the key to making the human mind try harder and risk everything to reach the stars, creating what they could only dream of elsewhere. But most of the immigrants wanted freedom and the opportunity to build their lives; they were entrepreneurs, eager to risk everything for the chance to be free. Those early settlers who risked the most and created the country's wealth made the United States the most dominant power on the planet.

The American economy is the backbone of the global financial system today, and US currency is the international exchange standard.

The military superiority of the armed forces is undeniable on the world stage. The United States spends more on financial assistance than other nations globally, thus ensuring the influence and cooperation of countries that need this assistance.

The United States is an undisputed leader in developing and applying the latest technologies, oil, and gas production, research, and growth in many scientific fields. It is a superpower with superior military, economic, and political power.

DEMOCRACY

The word "*democracy*" comes from the Greek word *dēmos,* meaning "people," and "κανόνες" —"rule," and is a collective decision-making process with equal participation.

There are many definitions of democracy, from Athenian democracy to socialism. Still, it always addresses equality, the principles of people's participation in political decisions, and the right to self-determination.

In ancient Greece, women and enslaved people had no political rights. In the city-states, power belonged to the citizens (free men). Various executive positions were appointed by lot or were elected.

The Roman Empire, with its elected government, was a model for Western civilization. The Roman aristocratic republic granted rights to the people's assembly. It elected officials, passed laws, declared war, or made peace. In reality, the power belonged to wealthy patricians who bribed voters to win elections.

One of the reasons for the Western Roman Empire's ruin was demographic degeneration associated with family institution crises. People stopped having many children, and its population began to be replaced by barbarians who moved into the territory. Historians of ancient Rome cited: "The celibacy and absence of children became more and more every day. Among married, children were considered a burden. As a result, the bulk of Italy's population was shrinking, and barbarians partially settled its desolate provinces."

Over time, the barbarians enlisted in the army and were then able to plunder and destroy Rome.

Perhaps the most critical advance of humanity is the freedom of choice. "Liberty, Equality, and Fraternity" was the motto of the French Revolution (1789–1799). It was an answer to absolutism: "God, King, Fatherland." In that trinity, the superfluous word was *king*. Although there were already atheists at that time, they were a minority. Atheists argue that faith in gods, spirits, the afterlife, or supernatural powers is self-deception. Scientific thought and empirical or physical evidence reigned. Still, people were not ready to give up their faith in God or turn away from the Fatherland.

The idea that people could create a perfect state structure with equal opportunities for all population segments appeared in different countries. After Britain suffered defeat in the war against the northern colonies in America, monarchs across Europe began to lose their influence. The French Revolution, led by the Jacobins, proclaimed the first French republic. The people ousted King Louis XVI in 1792. He was tried and sentenced to death. The guillotine executioner chopped the king's head off in Revolution Square.

The country's economy did not improve, and unrest began. The fight for power between the Girondists and the Jacobins resulted in a Jacobines' victory.

The civil war raged throughout the country. Prussian, Austrian, Spanish, and British troops invaded France. In a destroyed country, "repositories of abundance" were established, setting bread prices connected with wages. There was massive unrest, so the new government created an army and arrested people based on suspicion alone. A centralized dictatorship cleansed the government of nobility and essentially reigned with terror.

In 1795, extensive new political processes began. The Konvent sent Queen Marie Antoinette to the guillotine. There were so many executions the guillotine wasn't fast enough, so they resorted to mass shootings. The repression was against the noble class. Catholic churches were closed, and priests were repressed. Robespierre achieved the execution of Danton and other prominent Dantonists. Then Robespierre, St. Just, and others were executed without trial in 1794. The royalists rebelled, and a young general named Napoleon Bonaparte dealt with them. The terror and the executions continued.

Coalition forces of the British, Austrian, Neapolitan, Swedish, Russian, and Turkish armies were ready to invade. The Directory (interim government) welcomed General Bonaparte in Paris as a savior.

Bonaparte dissolved the Directory and created the Consulate of the five-member committee governing France during the "Reign of Terror." He proclaimed the senior government of France throughout the Napoleonic Empire. By suppressing all political freedoms, Bonaparte reorganized the administration from top to bottom, making his government strictly centralized.

Bonaparte was recognized as a life consul and, in 1804, was crowned emperor.

The Napoleonic Wars (1800–1815) redrew the map of Europe. Any war brings devastation and massive human casualties but can also bring economic domination.

In 1814, allied troops (the Russian army was the core of the allied forces) entered Paris. Napoleon was renounced and exiled to the island of Elba. Soon he fled and regained power again. He got his Waterloo and was sent to the island of Sant'Elena.

The consequences of the French Revolution, the Napoleonic Wars, and the freedoms won by the North American states did stir up a thirst for freedom and a desire to overthrow the monarchy, replacing it with a republic with universal equality.

EUROPE IN THE TWENTIETH CENTURY

This ill-fated century was the bloodiest in the history of humankind. Creative humanity invented modern weapons capable of mass killing large numbers of people. Tanks, bombs, poison gasses, and massive cannons did "great" jobs. Germany complained of a growing population's lack of living space and food shortages. The European states were divided into two military blocs looking for an occasion for war.

World War I (1914–1918) began with the assassination of Austrian Archduke Franz Ferdinand. The opposing camps were Germany, Austria-Hungary, the Ottoman Empire, and the Bulgarian state against the British Empire, the Russian Empire, and the French Republic.

World War I resulted in Russia the February Revolution of 1917, in which the monarchy was overthrown. More than twenty million soldiers and civilians were killed on both sides. Almost fifty-five million people were wounded or mutilated. In Germany, the November Revolution in 1918 replaced the federal constitutional monarchy with a democratic parliamentary republic and established the socialist Weimar Republic.

World War I collapsed four empires: Russian, Austria-Hungarian, Ottoman, and German.

The victors of World War I decided to create the League of Nations (1920–1946), an international organization dedicated to preventing military action and conflicts between states, ensuring collective security, resolving disputes between nations, and improving the quality of life on the planet.

Unfortunately, this newest system of international relations, as we know it now, was unable to keep the world from the bloody Second World War. Therefore, it transferred authority in 1946 to the new international guard of world order, the United Nations.

According to democratic principles, the United Nations united almost two hundred countries. Its headquarters, a vast complex of buildings, were built on the East River in Manhattan, New York. It employs forty-one thousand employees around the world. The UN created various committees and passed various rulings by democratic vote. Since the admission to the UN was open to all nations who agreed to adhere to the UN charter, any UN resolution adopted by a simple majority could condemn any world government for non-compliance with any rules. The UN convicted and punished many countries where human rights were violated. Some states, however, are slow to implement these essential orders.

Fortunately, at one time, there was enough reason to give the five permanent members—Great Britain, the United States, France, Russia, and China—the right to veto any resolution.

Today, some suggest this intergovernmental organization needs to be reformed because the members are unequal. The bureaucracy's growth contradicts the UN charter's goals and objectives. There is an increasing distrust of the legitimacy of the organization. Its authority in world politics has declined.

SOCIAL DEMOCRATIC MOVEMENTS

(Nineteenth and Twentieth Centuries)

By the beginning of the twentieth century, industrial capitalism had established itself in most European and North American countries. Social problems worsened, and labor movements sought democratic transformations. There were strikes, uprisings, revolts, and demonstrations—national liberation movements inspired by united international socialist parties—the Socialist International. Marxist ideas were spreading among the workers.

German philosophers Karl Marx and Friedrich Engels wrote *Das Kapital* and *The Communist Manifesto*, famous works of the nineteenth century. These works profoundly affected the socialist movements in the twentieth century. Many people from different countries joined and even headed social democratic movements.

In Russia, Aleksandr Ulyanov and his comrades purchased explosives and prepared an assassination attempt on the tsar. The plot was uncovered, and five conspirators were hanged. Ulyanov's young brother,

Vladimir Lenin (as he called himself), swore to avenge his brother. A sizeable disparate group of political emigrant revolutionaries from Russia gathered in Geneva and Zurich. They prepared revolutionary propaganda to send back to Russia. They published newspapers and leaflets and delivered them by trusted couriers to proxy contacts in Russia, intending to overthrow the Tsar.

After intense pressure from the revolutionaries, Tsar Nicholas II signed an abdication decree. Power was transferred to the body of the "provisional government" before the election of the constituent assembly.

The Russian Social Democratic Labor Party's radical wing, the Bolsheviks, broke with the domestic left-wing Mensheviks. The radical extremists made a secret agreement with the German General Staff to deliver the group of revolutionaries (the Bolsheviks) to Russia in a sealed wagon, passing through several neutral countries' borders. There were many speculations on payments made by the Germans to the Bolsheviks. Whether or not such transactions took place is unknown.

The October Revolution (or the Bolshevik coup) occurred in Russia in 1917. Russia emerged from the war, and the Bolshevik government made a separate peace treaty with Germany in Brest-Litovsk. The country repeated the French Revolution's entire path, with all its bloody horrors, civil war, terror, and devastation.

After Lenin's death, power was democratically passed to Joseph Stalin. This paranoid eastern despot and murderer held power for thirty years. He kept the semblance of democratic elections.

He was guilty of the repression and percussion of millions of people, responsible for more deaths than WWI and WWII combined.

In the Weimar Republic of Germany, the socialist movement started (1919–1933). Under the Treaty of Versailles that ended World War I, defeated Germany had to repay the victorious countries for damages. Germany was obliged to hand the winners their entire navy and significant territories. The nationalists wanted a reexamination of the humiliating treaty.

In 1929, the global depression hit. Vast sums of reparations weighed heavily on the country's economy. The German mark depreciated significantly. There were severe restrictions on all social programs.

The German National Socialist Workers' Party won six million votes in the democratically held parliamentary elections, and Hitler became the Reich chancellor.

The cruelest dictator in the world's history, the embodiment of evil, a paranoid psychopathic type, felt a constant hatred, especially toward Jews. Somehow during speeches, he immersed the crowd in a hypnotic state. Women, who adored their Fuhrer, handed him their children and offered themselves. They were ready to give their lives for him. The Nazis staged night torchlight processions, military parades, and noisy folk festivities. They were into mystical spectacles and the occult. On Kristallnacht, or the Night of Broken Glass, shop windows belonging to Jews were smashed. On the Night of Long Knives, Nazis killed former friends who helped Hitler to gain power (the group of Ryom). How did such an inadequate type change the nation and turn right-minded educated people into sadists and cold-blooded killers? How could a mediocre art student turn regular people into cruel killers of women, children, the elderly, and the infirm? What happened to the Germans' Christian humility and kindness, which led the dances at Christmas around the decorated tree, with tears in their eyes singing, *"O, Tannenbaum, O, Tannenbaum"?*

They were Homo sapiens, holding in limbic structure instincts of past animal nature. Gitler applies to those instincts.

The National Socialists coined Aryans (Indo-Iranian) and attached it to the Nordic race.

The Nazis' ideology proclaimed them as heirs to the pure Aryan race and bearers of the Aryan spirit. Judaism says that the Germans are the heirs of the Persian tribes that migrated to Europe many millennia ago. Aryans are ancient people of India and Iran who sacrificed to their gods.

The explanation for this unthinkable cruelty and thirst for killing innocent people lies more in mythology's realm associated with the new religion. Rejecting Christianity, Hitler promoted the theory of the superiority of a new race over the *Untermensch* or "under humans," those who are less than human.

Hitler was a bright speaker. "The German people, I ask you, do you need a total war? I, myself, will answer! Yes, you need it! At the same time, lazy and talentless Slavs have vast territories which they do not use. This injustice must be corrected. Every German must get a considerable land allotment, and the stupid and ignorant Slavs must work for the German master."

Such propaganda was met by the sleepy burghers (bourgeoisie) with patriotic enthusiasm.

Hitler fought in the First World War. He was hit by a chemical projectile, was gassed, and was in the psychiatric ward. He wanted to avenge everyone for the shameful defeat of Germany, especially the French. The Treaty of Versailles imposed various restrictions on Germany and did not allow Germany to equip its army openly. Since Hitler had militaristic aspirations and wanted to subdue Europe, he cooperated with Stalin, who had control of Russia and was not part of the European alliance. Hitler hated the Communists and severely persecuted them, but Stalin needed Hitler. Hitler knew this and played Stalin because he couldn't afford a war on two fronts. Firstly, he wanted revenge on all the Allies, which had brought Germany to its knees.

Shortly after coming to power, Hitler announced Germany's partial withdrawal from the Treaty of Versailles. Austria was annexed in 1938. In the same year, a part of Czechoslovakia's territory, the Sudetenland, was added. Also, the rest of the Czech Republic was occupied. After this, Germany annexed

Lithuania, then went after Poland. Allies of Poland, England, and France gave Germany a sharp rebuff. German and Soviet troops (according to the secret papers, called the Molotov-Ribbentrop treaty, signed between two counties) invaded Poland.

It was the beginning of World War II. Germany occupied Norway, Denmark, Holland, Luxembourg, and Belgium. Then Germans invaded France, and she capitulated. After the capture of Greece and Yugoslavia, Germany went after the former Soviet Union. A brutal German order was established in the occupied territories. Millions of people were killed.

The long and devastating war involved fifty-seven nations and killed millions of lives (estimated fifty to eighty million).

Stalin did not believe anyone. He trusted only one person—Hitler. This trust was based on a simple calculation. Their friendship was beneficial to both states. Germany and Russia could dominate the world if they remained united against a hostile Europe. German officers trained in Russian military academies. They held joint army exercises and performed battle exercises to prepare for territories in the Caucasus. Russia sent Germany oil, coal, ore, metals, grain, and many other things that Germany needed.

The Treaty of Non-Aggression, or the Molotov-Ribbentrop Pact, further contained secret protocols for Europe's power division. According to the Soviet treaty or non-aggression pact, the so-called Molotov-Ribbentrop Pact contained secret protocols on the division of influence in Europe.

According to protocols in 1939, the Soviet troops invaded Finland. But the Finns, under General Mannerheim's command, who built defensive strengthening, named The Mannerheim Line, fiercely resisted.

Soviet troops captured 11 percent of the territory of Finland. The Finns were forced to relocate thirty thousand people inland.

Not expecting a treacherous attack from a "friend" on June 22, 1941, Stalin hid from everyone in the early days of the war, waiting for his arrest.

In the first days of the war, the Wehrmacht's armed forces entered the country's interior and were thirty kilometers from Moscow by October.

In 1941, more than four million people were killed, cut off, and taken, prisoners. With manic suspicion and relying on German intelligence misinformation, the mediocre commander-in-chief Stalin arrested and shot the best and most experienced senior commanders.

The Holocaust in WWII estimated 6 million Jews' lives.

Hitler killed himself in May 1945. Stalin died in March 1953.

In 1970, a pamphlet was distributed among KGB officers, claiming the war between Russia and Germany was a mistake. The circular stated that the two most powerful nations in Europe, bound by a shared history, could unite the whole world under their influence.

Benito Mussolini was a *duce*, a dictator, and a leader of Italian fascists. As a Marxist socialist, he had longed to transform Italy. Obsessed with the Roman Empire's revival ideas, he abandoned socialist plans and created the National Fascist Party. Mussolini was democratically elected to parliament. In 1922, as the head of the fascist party, he organized a march to Rome. He became a dictator and joined a coalition with Hitler. He was arrested by British troops entering Italy in 1943 and later executed.

Francisco Franco was Spain's Caudillo (military leader, 1939–1975). He organized a military coup in 1936, which led to a civil war (1936–1939) between republicans and nationalists. Franco defeated the republicans and established an authoritarian regime. He was named *caudillo* (chief.) After World War II, Franco remained at the helm of Spain.

EUROPE AFTER WORLD WAR II

General Colonel Jodl signed an act of unconditional military surrender (May 7, 1945). Germany was occupied by the troops of the victorious countries: the USSR, Great Britain, France, and the United States.

Defeated Germany was isolated. The agreement of the Allied Powers provided for the creation of four zones of occupation. Subsequently, these zones formed two states: the Federal Republic of Germany (FRG) on the west and the Deutsche Democratic Republic (DDR) on the east.

Defeated Germany lay in ruins. The destruction of its infrastructure led the country to economic isolation. Millions of people were homeless. Without outside financial help, restoring the country's economy was impossible. The country and most of Europe needed economic recovery.

The elimination of the consequences and destruction of the war required the recovery of the economy. The Marshall Plan (Europe's post–World War II reconstruction program) was proposed by Secretary of State George Marshall in 1947. Fearful of communist influence in postwar Europe, the plan was directed at recovering the economy, industrial modernization, and eliminating barriers to Europe. The number of appropriations was about $13 billion.

The USSR and the established buffer socialist states (Warsaw Pact countries) refused to participate in the implementation of the Marshall Plan. Under the Marshall Plan, $3.12 billion was allocated in four years. Germany's leader Ludwig Erhard was considered the creator of *the* "new Germany." The nation quickly rose from the ruins and was called the "German Miracle." The appearance of the Deutschmark (1948) later became one of the most stable currencies in the world.

Material losses in WWII shocked beyond the imagination. The economy was pushed so far back.

However, there is still an opinion that war moves progress. New military industries will eventually enter the civil service. It may be accurate, but the psychological costs to society are never factored in.

EUROPEAN UNION

The idea of a European Union became loud after World War II. The Maastricht Treaty was legally formalized in 1992, when twenty-eight countries joined the economic and political union. The unification of European countries was perhaps an imitation of the United States, a union of rich and developing states. However, unification has revealed many contradictions. The EU is not a charity. Its budget of billions of euros comes from the contributions of participating countries. It is a disproportionate union. And the rich countries pay more but also benefit more from the overall market. This fissure was most seriously recognized after the UK referendum to leave the European Union (Brexit). The impact of the UK's exit has yet to be fully assessed.

The migrant crisis has caused another rift between Central and Eastern Europe. Germany's and France's mandatory quotas for migrants have sparked violent protests and the erection of cordons and borders. Despite the penalties and threats, most Eastern European and Baltic countries refused to comply with EU regulations. The differences in the various countries' economies, national currency exchange rates, per-capita incomes, and standing in parliament have all added to the growing problem of the European Union's survival.

German chancellor Angela Merkel led the movement to attract migrants from Africa and Arab countries. Today she admits that such an open-door policy was a mistake. Perhaps Mrs. Merkel and the tolerant democrats assumed that newly arriving migrants would fill low-paying and unprestigious jobs. Maybe they thought migrants would improve the demographics of old Europe, which is losing population. Children of migrants will have to become better educated to gain prestigious professions and become Europe's future. After all, the same happened in the United States. America in the nineteenth and twentieth centuries was flooded with waves of immigrants, most of whom were poor and looking for work and new opportunities. But the tolerant democrats in Europe were wrong. Waves of Mediterranean immigrants splashed onto European shores. And it turned out the migrants were not looking to work hard to get ahead. They came for the government benefits that a socialistic democratic European Union provided its citizens and, apparently, migrants.

Migrants demanded equal rights to housing, healthcare, construction of religious temples, and even the freedom to practice their religious Sharia law. They did not ask for anything. Instead, they demanded to be given things, arranging noisy processions and gatherings to get their way. They smashed windows and burned cars. They fought with the police and hid terrorists. They have turned a calm and quiet Europe into a nightmare, where terrified residents fear for their lives.

Does Europe have a future? Today, hardly anyone can say yes with confidence.

THE USA AND RADICAL DEMOCRATS

The United States of America is usually called merely America. It is a mighty bastion of democracy and equality for people of all races, genders, religious and sexual preferences. Many people want to be citizens of this country. The founder of the Democratic Party, Thomas Jefferson, probably would have rolled over in his grave after learning how far left the party's ideology had gone, from conservative to very liberal. The symbol of the US Democratic Party is a donkey. The forty-fourth president, Barack Obama, was the fifteenth Democratic president. He was a clear liberal but positioned himself as a centrist to get elected.

In Jefferson's time, the Democratic Party was the conservative party. The switch happened after Abraham Lincoln's presidency. In the nineteenth century, the Democratic Party, reflecting the Southerners' interests, supported slavery and advocated racial division. After the Confederates' defeat in the Civil War, the party declined for almost forty years.

The symbol of the US Republican Party is the elephant. Abraham Lincoln founded the party that often prevailed in state legislatures after the Civil War. In 1963, the charismatic and popular Democratic leader, President John F. Kennedy, was assassinated. Lyndon Johnson, the vice president, became president. He was tied to the Vietnam War and lost the presidential election in 1968. The Republican nominee, Richard Nixon, got 43.4 percent of the vote, defeating the Democratic candidate Hubert Humphrey. Nixon also won the next four years of the presidency. In 1976, Richard Nixon resigned in the wake of the Watergate scandal. The black mark gave a slight advantage to little-known politician Jimmy Carter. He was the Democratic governor of Georgia. He was not very popular and lost in 1980 to the fortieth President of the United States, Ronald Reagan. He was always interested in social issues and politics. He was a radio host, a trade unionist, and the thirty-third governor of California. He advocated reducing the state's economic control and fought against high taxes and government control. At first, Reagan was a member of the Democratic Party. He became a Republican in 1960, and as president, he called the USSR the Evil Empire and prepared for its collapse. Ronald Reagan said, "Government is not the solution to our problem; government is the problem." The Reagan economy (which Democrats contemptuously called Reaganomics) brought prosperity to the country. After two terms in the White House, Ronald Reagan ceded to George H. W. Bush, his vice president.

Under Bush Sr., the Berlin Wall fell (1989), and Germany was reunited. On December 25, 1991, the Soviet Union collapsed.

Bush made a ridiculous mistake when he swore to voters: "Read my lips, no new taxes." Shortly after, he signed a bill that raised taxes and thereby committed political suicide. He lost the next election to the unknown governor of Arkansas, Bill Clinton.

If George H. W. Bush Sr. had not made his tragic mistake, perhaps the United States' future history would have differed.

During a presidential debate (1992), George H. W. Bush, already clearly aware of his defeat, sadly addressed the audience: "He will come for your pockets." But no one listened to him. A young, energetic, smiling candidate who knew how to grab the audience's attention quickly handed out promises he knew he could not fulfill.

Much of America watched the debates on television. In one of the bars in the Wall Street area, I spoke to a young man who was a Bush Sr. supporter, judging by the conversation.

"Do you think this man, who talks like any socialist in Russia, who makes false promises during the elections, can beat Bush?"

"I do not doubt, Bush lied to the American people."

"Yes, he did. But how can you let such a person as Clinton be in power?"

"America is a stable country. It easily handles four years of someone like Clinton."

We were young and naive. Indeed, what could happen within a country like America? The Clintons arrived in the White House and made dramatic changes. Bill Clinton, the Democratic nominee, became the forty-second president of the United States. First Lady Hillary Clinton was appointed the head of a special commission on healthcare reform. Her reform failed catastrophically.

In 1996, the Clinton-Gore team successfully won a second term in office. The secretary of defense was directed to repeal the ban on gays in the military. In the face of widespread criticism, Clinton reversed his decision, but he found a way out. He just prohibited members of the armed forces from asking about sexual orientation.

The order became known as "don't ask, don't tell."

In 1998, the Clinton-Lewinsky sex scandal erupted. A forty-nine-year-old president and twenty-two-year-old White House intern Monica Lewinsky had multiple sexual encounters in the White House. When President Clinton obstructed justice and lied (under oath) before Congress, he was impeached. Bill Clinton escaped removal from the presidency, but he did lose his legal license and was fined ninety thousand dollars for perjury.

Hillary Clinton defended her husband in an interview on NBC's *Today Show*, saying: "This is the great story here for anybody willing to find it, write about it, and explain this vast right-wing conspiracy that has been conspired against my husband since the day he announced for president."

Using NATO, Bill Clinton launched a massive bombing campaign against the Serbs—without considering the evidence. Clinton later sent twenty thousand US troops to Bosnia to join NATO "peacekeepers." The media accused the president of using the attacks as a distraction from the sex scandal. Shortly before that, a film paralleled the events called *Wag the Dog* was released. The administration denied the similarities.

Yugoslavian officials estimated civilian bombing casualties as high as eighteen thousand.

The scandal, called Monicagate, was discussed in all media outlets. The president was shamed in front of the entire country. Under oath, he claimed no sexual contact with an intern at the White House. Lewinsky's famous blue dress was found to have traces of the president's sperm. Congress was forced to proceed with impeachment proceedings for perjury and contempt of court. The US House of Representatives impeached Bill Clinton. Still, he was acquitted on all counts of impeachment by the majority of Democrats in the US Senate, allowing him to finish his term.

Bill Clinton made a national television statement acknowledging his relationship with Monica Lewinsky. He described it as "inappropriate." In addition to Monica Lewinsky, several other women reported inappropriate behavior by Bill Clinton, going back to his time as governor of Arkansas.

Back in Arkansas, Bill first met Hillary Rodham Clinton. Hillary received her doctorate in law in 1973. An ambitious independent, Hillary was actively involved in politics. She was the most influential First Lady in the history of the White House.

During Bill Clinton's presidency, people called president Billary because the First Lady had much influence. An anecdote about Hillary's dominance goes like this: Bill and Hillary drove up to a gas station.

Hillary: "See the guy pumping gas in the cars? He was once my boyfriend."

Bill: "You see, if you married that guy, you'd be working at a gas station today."

Hillary: "If I married that guy, he'd be president today, and you'd be working at a gas station."

Although her attempt at healthcare reform failed, she continued to pursue ambitious goals. After Bill Clinton's second term ended in 2000, Hillary Clinton dreamed of getting back to the White House, but she knew she needed political experience. She probably decided to nominate Al Gore as the Democratic presidential candidate, and she would run for the US Senate.

Not wishing to run from Arkansas, the Clintons changed their residence to New York State. According to rumors, some "friends" bought them a house in an expensive New York suburb. After becoming a New York State resident, Hillary Clinton was elected senator. Al Gore lost in a tough fight for the presidency to George W. Bush. Al Gore justified his defeat on the low reputation of Bill Clinton, and Hillary's poor performance on universal health insurance was nicknamed Hillarycare. Hillary went on to easily win reelection to the Senate in 2006.

With the start of the 2008 presidential race approaching, Hillary was one of the most prominent Democratic candidates. Many voters were suspicious of the Clintons, suspecting nepotism, corruption, and even mafia connections. Hillary tried to change her public image of a cold and calculating lady to a softer, more maternal personality. When a new up-and-coming Democratic candidate, Barack Obama, entered the race, Democrats backed Obama, and Hillary Clinton was forced to declare support for Obama's candidacy. She later became the Secretary of State.

Barack Obama won the 2008 presidential election. He became the forty-fourth president of the United States (2009–2016). He was born in 1961 in Honolulu, Hawaii, USA. During his two terms in office, rumors about a possible forged birth certificate would make him ineligible to be president. Some people also claimed Barack Hussein Obama secretly professed Islam, although he claims to be a Protestant Christian. His father, Barack Hussein Obama Sr., is a Kenyan. His mother, Stanley Ann Dunham, counted English, Scots, and Irish among her ancestors. Obama's parents divorced. His mother remarried an Indonesian named Lolo Sutro. The family went to Jakarta, Indonesia. When Obama turned ten, he returned to Honolulu, where he lived with his mother's parents.

In his book *Dreams of My Father*, Obama recalled his childhood. During the presidential campaign, he admitted to smoking marijuana, using cocaine and alcohol at school. He described it as his lowest point morally. Obama studied at Columbia University and enrolled at Harvard University. He became the first African American editor of the Harvard *Law Review*.

In 1996, he was elected to the Illinois Senate. Eight years later, he became the fifth African American senator in the country's history.

He announced his plan to run for the presidency of the United States.

He raised $36.8 million in the primaries for the Democratic presidential nomination.

After a brief struggle, Hillary Clinton withdrew her candidacy, announcing her full support for Obama.

Obama and Vice-President Joe Biden won handily, even in traditionally Republican states. Obama's victory sparked instances of religious and racial hatred. African countries, as well as the countries of the Middle East, were euphoric. In 2009, Obama received the Nobel Peace Prize for "strengthening international diplomacy and cooperation between people."

In February of the same year, Obama signed an act injecting 787 billion dollars in economic aid to alleviate the global financial depression. In March of that year, the treasury secretary, Timothy Geithner, took additional steps to avert the financial crisis by publishing the Public-Private Investment Program for Legacy Assets, which bought legacy assets from banks to get them back on their feet. Obama also intervened in the burgeoning auto business, assuming loans for General Motors and Chrysler to reorganize their businesses. But both companies later went bankrupt and were sold to foreign investors.

The national debt rose to $17.2 trillion by February 2014. In 2009, Obama attempted dialogue with Arab leaders. He gave an interview to Arab TV Al Arabiya.

In further attempts to negotiate with the Muslim world, Obama sent a New Year's Eve video to Iran's people and leaders. In April, Obama spoke in Ankara, Turkey. In June of the same year, Obama spoke in Cairo, Egypt, calling it a "new era" between the Islamic countries and the United States. In March 2010, Obama opposed the Israeli government and Prime Minister Benjamin Netanyahu's plans to continue construction in East Jerusalem.

In the same year's midterm elections, the Democratic Party lost control of Congress. The same year, Obama passed a healthcare law. It's called The Affordable Care Act. It is nicknamed "Obamacare."

In August 2011, the Syrian Civil War broke out. Obama called on Assad to resign, and he ordered the deployment of US soldiers to Libya as part of NATO.

In 2012, he ran for a second term.

During his second term, the Obama-Biden team faced many problems that hurt the president's image. The healthcare system's failure and the scandal surrounding the Edward Snowden revelations, bombshell stories based on top-secret documents of NSA spying on American citizens. The attack on the consulate in Benghazi and four American citizens' deaths caused anger and irritation.

On December 23, 2016, the United States abstained from voting on United Nations Security Council Resolution 2334, which prohibited Israel from constructing buildings in Arab-populated territories violating international legislation.

The Obama administration sent a report to the US Supreme Court with the initiative to remove the ban on same-sex marriage. Same-sex marriage was legalized in 2015.

In the same year, Obama initiated a discussion on global climate control, leading to the Paris Treaty signing.

In November 2013, the Obama administration talked with Iran about preventing Iran from building nuclear weapons. Negotiations lasted two years, and the deal was approved by July 2015. This agreement envisages lifting sanctions in exchange for restrictions on creating nuclear weapons.

The deal received numerous criticisms from Republicans and conservative leaders, including Israeli prime minister Netanyahu.

In January 2016, President Obama announced four American prisoners' release due to complicated negotiations. The president explained to diplomats that Secretary of State John Kerry's negotiations had done everything they could to free the prisoners. The president gave Iran four hundred million dollars as part payment of $1.7 billion ($1.3 billion counts as a percentage of frozen funds). The settlement of money paid by the ousted shah of Iran for the supply of weapons that were never delivered blames the 1979 revolution in Iran. President Obama said, "The US is returning long-frozen funds to Iran." The "debt" to Iran was 400 million dollars plus 1.3 billion in interest. The frozen funds should not have been returned until a lawsuit over Iran's connection with a terrorist attack against American citizens was settled. As it was, the $1.7 billion payouts looked more like a ransom.

After paying Iran the first 400 million in cash, the remaining $1.3 billion was soon sent to Iran.

Despite numerous congressional hearings and demands for an investigation into this unprecedented scandal, there is hope for an impartial investigation. In the same year, Obama pushed through a nuclear deal with Iran. He also has normalized US relations with Cuba.

Barack Obama supported Hillary Clinton during the 2016 presidential race. Trump's victory meant the defeat of Barack Obama's legacy and the repeal of his reforms and transformations in eight years: healthcare reform, EPA regulation, foreign policy failures in Ukraine, the nuclear deal with Iran, and miscalculations in Syria. Hillary Clinton's victory meant all of his initiatives, legacy, and course for the country would be confirmed and continue.

Trump's victory was a significant setback for Barack Obama and the Democratic Party, a complete surprise, as they were confident of Clinton's victory. Obama's legacy has been shuttered and even under scrutiny as the lawlessness in the upper echelons of law-enforcement agencies has been revealed.

Heads of various agencies in the Department of Justice—FBI, CIA, State Department, DNI (Department of National Intelligence)—took place in nefarious activities to stop Donald Trump from being president and even bring him down from office. It has shown that they are committed to liberal values and serving the Democratic Party.

That was confirmed by the correspondence between FBI lawyer Lisa Page and former FBI agent Peter Strzok, with whom she was having an affair. Lisa was texting Peter, "POTUS [President of the US] wants to know everything…can Clinton lose?"

Strzok answered: "No. The odds are 100 million to zero. We're not going to let that happen."

Barack Obama knew everything.

Eventually, America will pay the price for those eight years' presidency of Barack Obama. Fear of riots and uprising in case of a nonelection of the first Afro-American presidency pushed those hesitant to vote for him.

MEET HILLARY CLINTON

Scandals arose around Hillary Clinton many times. She was involved in the infamous Watergate in the 1970s. She penned a critical memo during the indictment of Richard Nixon. Troopergate, Filegate, Travelgate, also during the Monicagate scandal, she supported her husband, who lied under oath. Hillary Clinton had many friends among Hollywood stars. The "famous" producer Weinstein, under investigation for sexual assault, donated $26,000 to her campaign. Prominent Hollywood star Kevin Spacey, also under investigation for sexual assault, is Clinton's friend. Many famous Hollywood stars were involved in the Hillary Clinton presidential campaign.

The Whitewater scandal is about a botched real estate deal with the Whitewater Development Company. The Clintons claimed they lost $25,000, tried to write it off on their taxes illegally, and obstructed the investigation. The Clintons' partner was Jim McDougal, owner of Madison Guarantee Bank. The bank went bankrupt, and its capital somehow replenished the accounts of Whitewater Development. The Whitewater case coincided with the 1993 year suspicious suicide of the Clinton family lawyer, Vince Foster. An independent prosecutor was appointed, but the case was closed in 2000 due to insufficient evidence.

The Clintons could be associated with many mysterious murders and suicides.

Hillary Clinton worked at the same firm that represented Jim and Susan McDougal, partners in the Whitewater investment deal. During her time as First Lady, Hillary was the subject of several investigations. The DOJ investigating the Whitewater case issued a formal subpoena to examine the Rose Law Firm's financial documents to determine if there was a conflict of interest. After two years of investigation, the records were found at the White House. Hillary Clinton is the only First Lady to be subpoenaed to appear before a grand jury. After numerous studies by independent counsels, a report was released about insufficient evidence of whether Hillary Clinton was involved in criminal offenses.

In May 1993, the Travelgate scandal broke. The White House Travel Office allowed some of Clintons' friends from Arkansas to travel for free even though they weren't White House employees.

In October 2002, a committee on government reform published a report regarding "problems with the presidential gifts system."

The report's summary findings included disclosing many gifts assessed at $260 or more. Expensive jewelry and gifts included Baccarat, Borsheim's fine jewelry, Ferragamo, Gucci, Hermes, Steuben, Tiffany, and more.

President Clinton's decision to accept gifts in his final year in office of close to $200,000 was questionable.

In March 1994, reporters discovered that Hillary Clinton, having invested $1,000 in cattle futures (1978-79), earned $100,000. They suspected a bribe. In 1996, an investigation was conducted into Hillary Clinton's role in firing White House staff. In 2000, an independent counsel reported that Hillary was involved in the layoffs. Expensive gifts were sent to the White House, and some of the furniture intended for the White House was sent to the Clintons' private home. The congressman who oversaw the investigation called Clinton's acceptance of the gifts "disturbing at best."

In January 2006, Hillary Clinton returned $28,000 worth of household goods.

Hillary Clinton had been preparing for the US presidency since 2003. In January 2007, she announced her participation, expressing her confidence in victory. The couple released a declaration of income, indicating that they had earned more than $100 million since 2000 thanks to books, speeches, and participation in various events—all because of Bill Clinton.

Hillary Clinton faced Senator Barack Obama of Illinois in the primary. After serving as secretary of state, Hillary became the first former First Lady to serve in the US Cabinet. The Democratic Congress supported Barack Obama. In June 2008, Hillary ended her campaign with a moving speech supporting Obama.

As a secretary of state, Clinton supported Lebanese rebels in killing Gaddafi and toppling his regime. Speaking about it, Hillary Clinton added with a smile: "We came, we saw, he died."

The civil war destroyed Libya, and everything that happened next is still the subject of litigation.

During the Syrian Civil War, Clinton and Obama persuaded president Bashar al-Assad to accept reforms. Yet, when government violence intensified, they changed their tune and suggested that Assad relinquish his presidency.

Hillary Clinton has always promoted what she called the Hillary Doctrine. She has advocated gay and human rights, strengthening the rights of women and minorities. In September 2012, the US diplomatic mission in Benghazi, Libya, was attacked. American ambassador Christopher Stevens and three other Americans were killed. The tragedy raised multiple questions about the safety of US consulates and officials. In October of that same year, Hillary Clinton took responsibility for the mistakes, explaining the inevitable consequences of war and chaos in these circumstances. She defended her actions during the incident but claimed she had no direct connection to the consular guard's specific details. Republican members of Congress accused the secretary of state of inaccuracies in her testimony of the attack.

Clinton erupted in a tirade, defending her position, adding, "What difference, at this point, does it make?"

In March 2015, there were reports that Clinton used a private server to send confidential and classified emails while she was secretary of state. That prompted more hearings on the attack on the American consulate in Benghazi. The FBI investigated the secrecy of the correspondence on her private server. The *New York Times* published an article on February 15, 2016, claiming that 2,100 emails stored on Clinton's server were classified. In February of the same year, Hillary Clinton said during a presidential debate with Bernie Sanders, "I never received nor sent any material that was marked classified." She claimed they were retroactively classified.

On July 5, 2016, FBI Director James Comey reported on the results of the investigation.

110 emails in 52 chains were marked as classified when sent and received. Eight of these chains of messages were classified as "completely classified" while they were being sent. Thirty-six chains of communications contained state-classified information at the time, with low secrecy. Separately from previous ones, about two thousand additional emails were labeled "high secrecy," which indicated privacy. The information about these was not secret when the messages were sent.

The investigation found that Clinton used her private server intensively, even while out of the country. The FBI noted: "It's possible that hostile actors gained access" to Secretary of State Hillary Clinton's private correspondence. But the FBI recommended the Department of Justice not prosecute her.

In June 2016, ex-president Bill Clinton flew to Phoenix on a private jet to meet with the head of the Department of Justice, Loretta Lynch. The conversation occurred at Phoenix Sky Harbor Airport aboard her private jet late at night. Asked about this late-night meeting, she said, "We talked about our grandchildren."

James Comey later said he had received instructions from Loretta Lynch to call the investigation into Hillary Clinton's emails a "matter."

Congress issued a subpoena demanding Hillary provide them with all the emails and servers. The documentary *Hillary America: The Secret History of the Democratic Party* was released in 2016. The film won the Golden Raspberry Award, awarded for the worst work.

Fox News contributor Dan Bongino traced the connection between Biden, Hillary, and Ukrainian oligarch Victor Pinchuk.

He pointed out that the politicians knew each other well and made good money in Ukraine. The prominent scandal erupted because of her unprotected personal email server to transmit confidential information. Hillary Clinton destroyed more than thirty-five thousand records.

The FBI launched an investigation. The FBI officers later destroyed the hard drive, contrary to the court subpoena.

James Comey released a statement announcing the end of the investigation into Hillary Clinton's private emails.

The world is still waiting for accountability and judgment on all actions this family deserves.

THE CLINTON FOUNDATION

Bill, Hillary, and their daughter Chelsea formed an organization called the Clinton Foundation in 2013, intending to "strengthen people's capacity in the United States and throughout the world to meet the challenges of global interdependence." Declared as a non-profit organization, the foundation was exempt from taxes but could collect money in the form of donations. By 2016, the foundation had raised $2 billion in donations from US and foreign corporations, governments, politicians, various groups, and individuals.

In 2016, the FBI released a statement investigating allegations of foundation corruption, possible financial irregularities, and potential misuse of funds by organizers.

Hillary Clinton was behind the US uranium deal with Moscow. The US House Permanent Select Committee on Intelligence and the House Committee on Oversight and Government Reform investigated a 2010 uranium deal with Russia. The sale involved transferring a Canadian uranium mining company, Uranium One, to control the Russian state corporation Rosatom. The Obama administration approved the transaction while

Hillary Clinton served as secretary of state. Clinton mysteriously gave 20 percent of US uranium to Russia. Rosatom subsequently bought a 100 percent stake in Uranium One. US regulators and a congressional committee hearing must review such a deal.

The FBI, under Director Robert Mueller, the same Mueller who became the special prosecutor in Russiagate, found out that Russia sent $145 million to the Clinton Foundation. After Russia announced its intention to acquire a significant stake in Uranium One, Bill Clinton received half a million dollars for a Moscow lecture. At the same time, Hillary Clinton was secretary of state.

In April 2015, Hillary Clinton announced her candidacy for the 2016 Democratic presidential nomination. She was, without a doubt, the most popular Democratic candidate. After defeating rival Bernie Sanders, she tapped Democratic Senator Tim Kaine as her running mate. She was defeated in November 2016 by Donald Trump.

For the Democratic Party, this defeat was the greatest tragedy. Democratic supporters, with champagne glasses and toasts prepared all over the country, wailed hysterically. Women sobbed, and men wept. Anyone would have thought it was the end of the world. Their lives lost all meaning. The Democratic Party leaders and established political elites pondered how to fight this unpredictable political newcomer who posed a clear threat to their comfortable existence. Trump's opponents weren't new in politics; they were battle-worn politicians. They were ready and able to fight for their power. This Deep State wanted Trump defeated by all means necessary.

The so-called Deep State is a collaborative group of top-level public servants who influence US politics. The Deep State and Hillary Clinton are responsible for commissioning British spy Cristopher Steele to draft a dossier on Donald Trump that they used to obtain a FISA (Foreign Intelligence Surveillance Act) warrant to wiretap the Trump campaign. James Clapper, former director of national intelligence, is credited with handing the dossier over to CIA Director John Owen Brennan.

Later it was discovered that Bruce Ohr, an executive with the Department of Justice, was involved in a conspiracy. Bruce's wife, Nellie Ohr, worked for GPS Fusion, the company that assembled the information for the dossier. Bruce Ohr shared this information with his boss, Rod Rosenstein, and was awarded $28,000.

Trump's presidency undeniably posed a threat to the heads of the security agencies, as he promised in his campaign speeches to "drain the swamp," meaning put an end to cronyism and corruption in Washington.

Trump's nomination directly threatened the DNC (Democratic National Committee). Everything became shaky and unpredictable, as proven by a letter Hillary Clinton sent to Donna Brazile, the head of the DNC at the time: "He [Trump] can hang us on the noose. You'd better do something about it now."

Even Hillary's robust foundation or friends couldn't get her into the White House.

IDEOLOGIES

In the United States, there are only two main political parties: Democratic and Republican. The other parties are not popular enough to pose a real threat. The Founding Fathers of the country drafted a constitution that provides checks and balances, preventing the concentration of power and eliminating tyranny. The country prospered, attracting more and more immigrants seeking freedom and new opportunities. Free enterprise, the cornerstone of America, has made it the world's wealthiest and most powerful country. The Thirteen Colonies declared independence in 1776. In less than 250 years, the country has overtaken all other countries to become the most influential world leader.

What other economic systems can produce such a state reactively in a short period? The capitalist economic model is based on private property, legal equality, and freedom of entrepreneurship. This model created an excellent market economy.

Critics of capitalism say it concentrates political influence into the hands of a relatively small class of wealthy capitalists who exploit working people. Defenders of capitalism say that the free market only produces a better product with its competitive and economic forces and lower pricing. It promotes, innovates, and distributes income among the more hardworking and talented. It increases economic growth and prosperity, ultimately serving the good of all society. It is human nature to work hard, and we all want to create wealth for our descendants. When something belongs to the government, it belongs to no one. And no one is willing to work as hard as they do for themselves—and only if the government does not interfere with too many regulations and taxes.

When the government is driven by ideology, introducing new bills to help the non-working part of society, or to other states, to protect the environment, or new taxes on business, every time someone has to pay for everything. Enterprises working for a profit must see predictable results. Any business will fight for freedom and independence from government interference or permanently move the business elsewhere. Everything has its price.

Civil wars always cost lives. The French Revolution destroyed the country. The revolution in Russia was even worse. Look at Venezuela and North Korea, China and Vietnam. We can add Haiti and South Africa, where people live in misery.

Europe's liberal democratic ideas are moving toward an enormous crisis. The US Democratic Party has moved far to the left. They range from centrist to ultra-radicals. Ultra-radicals aspire to power in the hope of promoting their ideas to life while not forgetting about their own well-being. The ideas of capitalist society disgust them in principle. Being socialist communists, in essence, they stand up for universal equality, the division of property of the rich, free treatment, education, food, and existence.

Achieving all this coveted existence is possible only by destroying the existing system. A country such strong economically and militarily as the United States can only be destroyed from within.

Ultra-radical Democrats are striving to change the existing state structure of the United States. Changing the country's constitution and establishing a socialist system that will equal all sections of the population's rights is necessary. That is the dream of the ideologists of communist ideas, Karl Marx, Friedrich Engels, Vladimir Lenin, and Joseph Stalin. It does not matter that such attempts led to catastrophic consequences. Neo-socialists know how to build a bright future of universal equality. The country must accept millions of refugees from third-world countries, which will increase devastation and hostility among the indigenous population and become a reliable support for the party that helped them.

Democrats, a liberal political party, accuse opponents of political extremism, white supremacy, and "domestic terrorism" (the so-called storming of the Capitol building). On the side of the democrats, new immigrants, liberal women, social networks, mass media, most African Americans (BLM, ANTIFA), and LGBTIQ+, it functions as an umbrella term for sexuality and gender identity.

To neo-Democrats, there is only one way; this country must be destroyed. The economy must be ruined, the country's population must be divided into warring clans, the law-abiding population must be intimidated, and crime must be encouraged. Family institutions, marriage, and other ties must be ridiculed, and all sorts of vices must be stimulated and introduced into the public consciousness. The primary attention should be directed to the education of the younger generation, which is easier to inspire with new ideas of sexual freedom and the right to use light drugs.

So much similarity to Lenin's ideas of destroying the existing order, eliminating all the rich, and building a new socialistic dream state.

Maybe there, democrats have the idea? Destroy everything to the ground and create a new, opponent-free world on it. On their way are the capitalist structure of the country and the republicans, the conservative political party, interfering with the wishes for reforms. GOP's for traditional American ideals and values: freedom, equality, democracy, individualism, the right to private property, belief

in one's abilities, patriotism, and religiosity; these are all things neo-socialists must fight and win.

Destruction of the family institution, unwillingness to have children, sexual perversions (debauchery, vices, homosexuality). The history of our species knows examples of similar catastrophic destruction. Such is the thousand-year history of the great Roman Empire. The crisis in the army and the economy, the lack of a strong leader, and the assimilation of barbarian tribes that did not have culture and the Roman ideology (most of the army was formed by barbarians). The ruin of the middle class, the destruction of spirituality and patriotism, and increased corruption. Crisis in all areas, including literature, art, and architecture.

For liberal democrats, capitalism and free-market economics are risky propositions not worth betting on. Democrats envision a beautiful life of comfort and ease provided by the government. Rather than spend young age working hard and prospering to ensure satisfaction in old age, democrats think young people should enjoy all the pleasures of life now.

Or it could be a bright idea to bet on the catastrophic ruins of the county's economy, buy everything at the bottom prices, and then re-establish law and order to become incredibly rich.

They want to spend the wealth of the future today. This socialist ideology seems a simple, accessible, and easy way to get power. All the advantages and opportunities are available to well-spoken people, promising well-being to ordinary and simple people. They promise the people everything for help get power and then love to live off the fat of the nation's wealth. They pit the people against each other. It is easier to blame others and vote for those who would take and share with a divided country. They impose taxes on the capitalist captains, and businesses make them understand they can make money, but they must pay generously.

Before Trump's triumph in 2016, it seemed the United States was flying into a bottomless pit of socialist ideas. The platform of the Democratic Party was becoming more radical. Newly elected members of Congress are closer to communists than to socialists. They insist on raising taxes on the wealthy up to 70 percent or even 90 percent (above a certain income level). They call for free Medicare for everyone, free schools and colleges, and a guaranteed income whether you are working or not.

For many years, the socialists have been running the White House. After eight years of Bill Clinton, there were eight years of Republican George W. Bush. During the Bush presidency, we saw the country in danger and at war. The monstrous terrorist attack of September 11, 2001, was planned and paid for by Osama bin Laden, a wealthy man of the radical Islamic terrorist group al-Qaeda.

Nineteen suicide bombers with sharp knives hijacked four passenger planes and flew them into symbols of American democracy: the World Trade Center, the US Capitol, and the Pentagon.

The first plane crashed into the 110-story South Tower. At first, no one understood what had happened. No one could believe that it was so easy for some terrorists to hijack a passenger plane and fly it into the heart of Manhattan to blow up the WTC.

As soon it was clear this was a planned terrorist attack, the Secret Service flew President George W. Bush out of Washington, DC. The military offered to shoot down the second plane flying to Manhattan. The president was supposed to give the order, but George W. Bush couldn't do it, explaining that there were American citizens on board. Fifteen minutes later, a second plane rammed into the North Tower.

A third plane crashed into the Pentagon, which houses the US Department of Defense. One hundred twenty-five people in the building and sixty-four airline passengers were killed.

A fourth plane hijacked by suicide bombers headed toward the Capitol, but heroic passengers aboard the airliner resisted the terrorists, and the aircraft crashed into an empty field. More than three thousand people were killed in that terrorist attack.

Ideologies have consequences.

NEW-OLD RELIGION: DEMOCRACY

Homo sapiens are all different. Human brains are not the same.

Human brains depend on the genes obtained from their parents. It depends on place of birth, physical and physiological characteristics, upbringing, education, habitat, wealth in the family, country, climate, religion, culture, and whether the person lived in a favorable environment or not.

Even living in the same society, people feel and perceive information differently. To one, everything that happens seems reasonable and justified; to another, it seems false and abusive. We argue until we are hoarse, join opposite communities, and are ready for anything to prove our case.

That is true for everyone except those who have chosen a career in politics. The ambitious business of being a politician is highly attractive and generously rewarded. Personal likes and dislikes do not matter. The main thing is to choose the right side of the winners and loudly declare commitment to this ideology. In case of failure, there is always the opportunity to admit mistakes and delusions or go over to the winner's side.

Since the mid-nineteenth century, the Democratic Party has shifted towards socially liberal and progressive positions. Accordingly, the electorate of the party has also changed. After struggling to preserve slavery, the Democratic Party has become a so-called advocate for the poor and minorities. Democracy is about majority rule. The majority dictates to the opposition. Even if the opposition is 49.9 percent, it must live by the declared majority's provisions. It is probably unfair, but up to now, no one has come up with an ideology or a system that can replace a democratic society. Democracy is not an invention of modern society. Humanity is familiar with this from the days of ancient Greece and the Roman Republic. Those democracies differed from the present because they served a particular class. Enslaved people and women could not participate in legislation or debate. As for homosexuality, it was not unusual or forbidden. In ancient Greece and Rome, it was a common occurrence. The Abrahamic religions that conquered much of the world had a negative attitude toward homosexuality, as indicated in Sodom and Gomorrah's destruction.

Democratic leaders in America today dream of socialism. They push universal equality through mass media, educational institutions, and Hollywood. They think it's a model system for the world. So far, they have driven the country into enormous debt. America remains the most potent country globally, the one the entire civilized world looks to for protection from terrorists. What made America gloriously and mighty was its freedom and the free-market system. President Trump was trying to Make America Great Again" MAGA"—the country he loves so much and is sincerely proud of. Democrats hate everything Trump did and are doing everything they can to prevent him from returning. It seems they want to make America miserable and dependable on union with other countries.

The country can vote President Trump back into office, but the democrats confronted every one of his initiatives. They will lie, cheat, and do anything possible not to elect him as a president.

Democrats, to achieve that goal, are ready to ruin the whole country. For them, only the way to get rid of republicans, get the majority in both parts of Congress, and make changes in the Constitution is to let them be the only party ruling forever.

Well, it's understandable. Democrats want to change the Constitution to become the most powerful and, even better, the only leading party in the United States. They want to save their power. Realizing that the republicans are supported by almost half of the country's population, they are forced to resort to cardinal changes in the public consciousness. The collapse of the economy, the impoverishment of the population, the criminalization of public consciousness, racial intolerance, the destruction of family values, the upbringing of the younger generation in contempt for the ideals of the older generation, and sexual permissiveness will lead to the destruction of the American way of life.

Who remembers the communist anthem "The Internationale"?

> *Get up, damned,*
> *The whole world of hungry and slaves!*
> *Boils our minds indignant*
> *And ready to fight to the death.*
> *We will destroy the whole world with violence*
> *To the bottom and then*
> *We are ours, we will build a new world,*
> *Who was nobody – he will become everything!*

Maybe here, democrats got the idea? Destroy everything to the ground and create a new, opponent-free world on it. They are ready to play big.

Democrats are counting on young extremism and suggestibility to allow sixteen-year-olds the right to vote. They also want to let more illegal immigrants inside the country and give them the right to vote.

The speaker of the House of Representatives, Nancy Pelosi, said, "Crossing the border is not a crime."

In some states, illegal immigrants can vote in local elections. In some cases, they can get free medical care too.

A great fuss was raised among democrats and a prominent left mass-media force when Trump proposed temporarily shutting down emigration from six hostile Muslim countries. Some of the illegal immigrants are Muslim. Muslim communities, even in this country, follow Sharia law. They are opposed to Hollywood's values but vote democratic because democrats and Hollywood want to change America's values.

Nancy Pelosi said about Joe Biden, "This is a president who has a great vision for our country. We see that every day. He has vision and values that go with it—he is a president who has the knowledge and, therefore, judgments about policies that can work. So again, God has blessed us with the timing of this presidency and this person, who is making such a tremendous difference in the lives of the American people."

So again, God has blessed us with the timing of this presidency and this person, who is just making such a tremendous difference in the lives of the American people."

Joe Biden was Barack Obama's vice president for two terms. If something goes wrong, democrats will blame Joe Biden for all the sins and consequences of his pursuit of a policy of such entire destruction of the United States.

Nancy Pelosi is right; this is precisely the kind of character that destructive policies. But even Obama, with all his popularity, would not dare to follow the current policy of the Democratic Party in the United States needs.

Democrats are ready to play big.

Hollywood, with its traditional liberal views, united against Trump's policies. Once a year at the Oscars, hosts' performances reject traditional American values and call for more anti-capitalistic heroes. The awards are given to films that attack the values that made this country great. They demand universal equality, higher taxes, and more regulations, hoping it won't affect their luxurious lives.

Hollywood and democrat elites accuse Trump of being a showman, a misogynist, a Kremlin agent, lacking a presidential style. They applaud and participate in the most vulgar and heinous human vices. They burned American flags in front of the White House.

Trump's style may be different from the politically correct deceitful politicians. However, he is accessible to average Americans and shares their traditional values and beliefs about border security, immigration laws, and the preservation of great America.

The elite has privileges, opportunities, wealth, and security, ready to do anything in the fight against President Trump, who is dangerous to them. The US population growth is mainly due to immigrants from

Latinos, Muslims, and African countries sympathetic to socialism. Democrats have pitted women against men. Women, who have traditionally been integral in perpetuating societies as wives and mothers, are now competing with men. These rights were won thanks to suffragettes, who achieved women's rights in the 1920s. Women began to receive a decent education and joined men in fields previously considered exclusively male. In the beginning, cooperation was healthy. Today feminists see women's progress as competition or even a war of the sexes. They criminalized unavoidable flirting present in the contact between men and women.

There is a widespread attack on the presumption of innocence, the basis of Western jurisprudence. Women come up with slogans like *"we believe survivors,"* meaning all women have to claim they were sexually harassed, and the man is presumed guilty. Flirting has become a criminal offense. The confirmation hearings for the Supreme Court's new member, Brett Kavanagh, are proof of this. Judge Kavanagh was accused of sexual assault decades after the supposed event. The accuser did not remember when, where, who she was with, or how she got home, but she was sure there must have been an assault.

President Trump's haters have flocked to power. Feminists in the United States can be incredibly aggressive. At President Trump's inauguration, thousands of women protested by wearing pink caps on their heads in the shape of female reproductive organs. In the US Congress, new young members of the Muslim Democratic Party—Rashida Tlaib and Ilhan Omar—and the radical Alexandra Ocasio-Cortez (AOC) got the idea the world would end in twelve years unless emergency actions were taken. AOC developed a new concept called the "Green New Deal." If implemented, this legislation would prohibit all kinds of energy. It would ban airplanes and cars. It would even try to limit cow farts. Their official communist slogan is "Everything is free and for everyone. Regardless of whether a person works. Medicine, education, and a high salary for all." Of course, no one knows from where all the money will come.

Trump calls for America to return to greatness (Make America Great Again—MAGA). He wants to end uncontrolled immigration through the southern border and build a wall. Of course, the project drew fierce resistance from the Democratic Party, for whom an uncontrolled influx of immigrants guarantees an electoral majority. Democrats won more votes in the midterm congressional elections, thus becoming a majority in the House of Representatives.

They now control the seat of the Speaker of the House of Representatives and most committee chairs. They aim to eliminate Trump's possibility of being elected to a second term or get him impeached. They don't hide their intentions. So far, democrats can't do it. Trump said he was ready to run for a second term during his inauguration. Everything that democrats achieved with such difficulty was crumbling before their eyes.

In May 2017, Rod Rosenstein, deputy chief prosecutor of the Justice Department, advised President Trump to fire FBI Director James Comey. Rosenstein harshly criticized Comey for the inadequate investigation into Hillary Clinton and her private server used for classified correspondence during her tenure as US Secretary of State.

The president of the United States has the right to fire any civil servant. It turned out to be a simple setup. The fallout from Comey's firing was not long in coming. As the Americans say, "all hell broke loose." The media, proudly calling themselves the Fourth Estate, put much pressure on Trump. They blamed him for all the deadly sins. Almost every news outlet and publication, except Fox and several talk shows, spread rumors defaming President Trump and his family. They declared war. Trump called all the attackers "fake news." Despite the Trump administration's successes in almost all politics and economics, bullying was not interrupted for a day.

Democrats in Congress and the Senate have demanded an investigation into the 2016 election because they said there was a reason to suspect Moscow of helping Trump win the election. The Justice Department created a commission of special prosecutors represented by former FBI director Robert Swain Mueller III. Simultaneously, the attorney general, Jeff Sessions, recused himself from the probe, claiming to have had ties between the Trump campaign and Russia. Sessions transferred all the authority to create the commission to his deputy, Rod Rosenstein.

Robert Mueller's commission immediately began work by hiring seventeen people, thirteen of whom were registered democrats.

Trump called the commission's work a "witch hunt." Trump tweeted: "Based on false accusations related to the wiretapping of Trump team, on Carter Page, foreign-policy adviser of election campaign fabricated allegations by FBI, fake 'dossier' manufactured by an English spy Cristopher Steele and paid by 'Crooked Hillary." DNC cheating on using FISA Court warrant to spy for my presidential campaign."

It's not that hard to get. What is the FISA Court? That's a federal court issuing a permit to wiretap foreign spies inside the US. This permit is provided for ninety days and can be extended by a judge for a subsequent period if necessary. The judge asks for confirmation as to whether all the statements listed in the request are correct, and the presenter of the account raises his right hand and says yes. That's where the hearing ends.

Russiagate began with James Robert Clapper, Jr., director of national intelligence and an Obama appointee. Clapper secretly met with retired British spy Christopher Steele. Why English and not American? US law forbids spying on American citizens without a FISA court judge issuing an order. Christopher Steele and the private investigative company Fusion GPS fabricated a dossier on Trump and his aides to show how he met with Kremlin emissaries to negotiate support for the presidential race. That dossier was made for Hillary Clinton, who paid for it and intended to use it during the presidential campaign. Without the dossier, the FBI's deputy director, Andrew McCabe, refused to get the FISA court warrant. Without the dossier and FISA warrant, the FBI could not listen to Trump's team's conversations.

Clapper passed the coveted dossier to another participant in the plot, the CIA director, John O. Brennan, who passed it on to the FBI.

Cristopher Steele received a monetary reward for work and an unverified and unconfirmed dossier to become irrefutable evidence to obtain a FISA court warrant. The FBI began listening to conversations between US presidential candidate Donald Trump and his entourage. Trump called this coup the Russian Hoax.

Mueller's investigation, called Russiagate by the press, cost more than $30 million and took two years. Prosecutors questioned more than five hundred witnesses, the paperwork from which amounted to more than a million pages of documents. The four-hundred-page report was released on March 22, 2019, and sent to the new attorney general, William Barr. The redacted report was published. The main conclusion made by Mueller's team: "investigation could not establish that members of the Trump campaign conspired with the Russian government in its election interference activities. The investigation also could not establish a violation by the president."

Democrats of all ranks and positions erupted in outrage, accusing Mueller, Barr, and Trump of conspiring to mislead the American people. Democrats demanded that Congress require Barr and Mueller to testify under oath and give them a full, unredacted report to review for themselves. Mueller refused to appear before Congress, but Barr promised to submit a comprehensive report quickly. That did not satisfy the democrats, who had been deceived in their expectations and demanded Mueller testify, hoping to convict him of lying. Mueller's report was submitted to Congress. Nothing changed.

On May 29, 2019, Mueller announced his resignation from the DOJ, and the special prosecutor's office shut down at a public press conference. He repeated that Russia was guilty of involvement in the American election process. Then, unexpectedly, he refuted the findings of his report: "If I were sure that Trump had not committed a crime, I would have said so."

Mueller also confirmed that he would not testify further to the US Congress. That caused a storm of emotions from all sides. Everyone was trying to guess precisely what Mueller wanted to say and why he made this statement contrary to his report.

It seemed victory was close for the democrats. House Speaker Nancy Pelosi looks strange, not controlling her speech and waving her arms. Her steady mate, Senate Minority Leader Chuck Schumer, looking bizarrely sideways like a hyena, reminded the hotheads that the chances of impeachment were close to zero. Democrats demanded that their leaders immediately begin the process of impeachment and force Mueller to testify to Congress. But maybe they thought such action would damage the president's reputation and reduce his re-election chances in 2020.

In close quarters, Nancy Pelosi expressed a desire to see the president "in prison." It became public. The left in America rejects traditional morals and family values. The new generation of the left has very liberal views of the world. New Americans, people who, for various reasons, could not succeed in their homelands, hope to get all the benefits in the USA. They intend to enjoy life in this country and show discontent because their expectations differ from reality.

Socialists persuade people to be dissatisfied with everything. They want everyone to think it's good to take away from the rich and divide among the poor. Democratic ideas about equality and socialism are finding more and more adherents. Over time, migrants become immigrants, get citizenship, and live in the country quite comfortably, but not everyone can fit into new circumstances, hard work, and financial obligations. Even a prosperous state doesn't have to rush to the rescue immediately. Everyone should learn to fight for their place under the sun, not wait for handouts.

In 1935, the social welfare program appeared in the United States. President Franklin Delano Roosevelt pushed a direct--assistance system for those in need through Congress. In 2018, the US government spent roughly $1 trillion on welfare programs. The excellent idea of helping the poor has turned into a welfare trap. The personal responsibility to work and earn money for the family has disappeared. In 1980, young people, many African American women, were the recipients of the welfare program, getting benefits after having babies out of wedlock. If the child stayed in school after the age of eighteen, the family continued to receive benefits, in fact, for the rest of the mother's life.

Where could she go to work after forty-five or fifty years old, having no profession or work experience? These incomplete families inhabited entire areas. The government pays for an apartment, food, health insurance, and provides some cash. This system ruined more than one generation, putting them in a "welfare trap," as it was called later.

Drugs, crime, alcohol, and gangs flourished. Food stamps were sold for cash to purchase drugs.

Socialists did interfere in human community development's natural evolutionary process; it triggers different processes using criminal organizations' systems. A lack of desire to fight for a place in life pushes people into dependency, poverty, and addiction to drugs and alcohol.

A few years ago, liberals realized that and agreed to do something about such a horrible situation. But that would not stop the process. Those hooked on welfare, generations of dependents, demanded even more privileges. The government continues to pay off not only food stamps but free housing, free medicine—offers to those willing to work, available positions in government offices. European colonists and entrepreneurs built and improved the USA, and those wishing to find their dreams on American land worked hard. No one offered them any welfare or any other social programs. They learned how to survive in the harsh conditions of developing a new continent.

Today's democrats do not know how to build a prosperous country. They think the state should solve every problem. They dream about a socialist state. They wish to build a country where welfare exists—it is socialism. The government decides everything—it is socialism. Free medicine for everyone—is socialism. Democrats believe in socialism.

As we all know by now, this system does not work. Not in Russia, Cuba, Venezuela, Eastern European countries, or elsewhere.

Eight years of the democratic Clintons in the White House destroyed the image of the presidency. Clinton brutalized the country's economy by sending production to other countries through the North America Free Trade Agreement. He made war within Yugoslavia, hoping to distract people from his sex scandal with Monica Lewinsky.

Republican president George W. Bush piled on the debt with eight disastrous years of military intervention.
Under democratic president Barack Obama, with Hillary Clinton as secretary of state, insurance companies made good money on Obamacare. The economy became a garland of bubbles, and the stock market collapsed. President Barack Obama ordered the printing of as many dollars as banks needed. The war in Libya, the killing of Americans in Benghazi, and the Arab Spring brought chaos to the Middle East. The prominent scandal of Obama with Hillary Clinton as Secretary of State is still waiting for his whistleblowers—the sale to Russia of 20 percent production of American uranium reserves.
That involved the corruption of all branches of power structures and is waiting to be exposed. Now in the wake of Russiagate, the democrats are afraid of exposure. President Trump allowed the new attorney general of the Department of Justice to declassify records he found necessary to clarify the Mueller Commission's investigation circumstances. New secret documents are being made public.
The democrats and the press expressed extreme concern about an "ill-considered stupid decision, capable of creating a threat to national security."

Naturally, democrats in Congress and the mass media unleashed a barrage of accusations against President Trump's decision. They demand admission to all materials of "Russiagate."

For years, the Democratic Party in the White House has helped spread socialist ideas in schools, universities, Hollywood, social networks, and media. Democracy, the rule of the majority, inevitably leads to dictatorship.

The US Democratic Party became a socialist party. Bernie Sanders, an ardent socialist, is again trying to run for president. In 2016, he fought successfully against Hillary Clinton but had to concede to her by the DNC order. If anything happens to Joe Biden, Sanders will likely be the democratic primary candidate in the 2020 presidential election. Or someone else who is even more left.

In his book *States*, the Greek philosopher Plato argued that excessive democracy inevitably leads to tyranny. The Roman Republic ended with the power of Caesar. City-states that had elected systems for senior leadership positions sooner or later dissolved into corruption, and internal conflicts fell under authoritarian regimes.

The great French Revolution spilled rivers of blood and ended with the imperial power of Napoleon. Once again, Europe was burning the fire of wars, and only the steadfast resistance of Russia stopped the conquest of the continent when the Allies defeated Napoleon's army at Waterloo.

The social-democratic movement in Russia destroyed the tsarist rule and radicalized Marxists in communist governments as the "dictatorship of the proletariat." Joseph Stalin, who succeeded the late Vladimir Lenin, constructed what was in his vision *as* a communist paradise.

Tens of millions of victims of the wildest totalitarian regime built the GULAG (concentration camps) in the name of a "bright future of free people."

Today Russia did not learn anything and continues its socialist path.

We remember what happened in China under Secretary Mao. We remember Pol Pot's bloody regime.

After World War I, the newly resurgent Weimar Republic splashed out on German politics' crest with a National Socialist Party led by Adolf Hitler.

Never before has humankind experienced such destruction of the human race. Not in bad dreams or fantasies; horror writers could not imagine the ghouls that suddenly appeared in reality.

Today's European cities are open to those who wish victory for the new barbarians. The road to hell is paved with good intentions. A benevolent social-democratic Europe bridges its way, believing tolerance and liberalism are the keys to a bright future.

So far, the United States is the last bastion against the socialist democrats. The besiegers did not even doubt the much-desired and well-thought-out strategy of capturing the crumbling target. Hillary Clinton was supposed to be the battering ram that would break through the Founding Fathers' wall of 1776. No one doubted the victory. If Clinton could get to power, the United States of America as we know it already would change.

But a miracle happened. Donald Trump won. He stands like a rock and builds America, where he was born and is the country he sincerely loves. Only a man like him has endured constant attack and slander from the high tribunes and media for four years.

God bless America and you, Mister President!

GRATITUDE

Thanks to everyone who helped me work on this book.

Numerous sources were used in this book's creation:

Sigmund Freud: *Totem and Taboo* and *Man Moses: The Psychology of Religion*.

Torah; Prophets; Scriptures; New Testament.

Charles Darwin: *The Origin of Species by Natural Selection*.

My sincere gratitude to those who helped me search for various materials, from social networks, journalism, mass media, historical, science research publications, and many other open sources.

SHIMON GARBER

Homo Sapiens

A collection of essays

VOLUME II

PREFACE

At first glance, it may seem that the beginning of the second book contradicts the logic of hominids' appearance in the first book, printed separately in 2019. In reality, in the second book, *Homo Sapiens II*, some other's version of higher primates' possible development led to the emergence of a new species—hominids. Our knowledge of human society's development depends on new findings and studies of thousands and thousands of scientists. They dedicated their lives to discovering the past and possible ways of developing our species, *Homo sapiens*.

According to Wikipedia, hominids include advanced families of large primates, giant apes (gorillas, orangutans, chimpanzees), and humans. Modern anthropologists attribute these species' development to hominids based on two simple criteria: walking on two legs and a tooth-jaw apparatus (lack of pronounced fangs, the shape of a dental arc, and shortened jaw). Hominids' brains have a volume of 600 cubic centimeters or more (unlike the brain of primates with 300 cubic centimeters). Why do we need to know and study the origins of our ancestors, hominids? In addition to the scientific and cognitive interest in man's background and evolution, it is hidden in millennials' depths and could explain some problems we experience.

Homo sapiens is a biological creature with a sufficiently developed brain that has turned our species into humans. The possession of spoken language has allowed our species to invent writing, create civilizations, religions, science, culture, and ensure survival by creating food reserves.

Our species has been destroying their kind in wars for thousands of years. They hid behind religious, moral, or other reasons, using the strongest's rights. The horrendous cruelty of wars not only did not become more civilized but, on the contrary, the number of brutally destroyed increased with each century. The invention of more and more perfect weapons of murder, most wild and mercilessly, when the count is already reaching hundreds of thousands of lives and approaching millions destroyed at once, is not a tragedy of humanity but a triumph of the victors.

How and why does this happen to our civilized world? The answer lies within ourselve, or rather, in our brains. In our subconscious (in the limbic system of the brain), we have remained a natural part of the animal world, striving to protect ourselves at any cost and destroy the one who in our brain is a threat to our existence. *Homo sapiens,* in the past, have been cruel animals. Wild ways to destroy the enemy are not unusual. Under certain circumstances (famine, rituals of cannibal triumph over the vanquished), perhaps the spirit of a wild creature of the animal world returns.

The nineteenth, twentieth, and twenty-first centuries are vivid proof of this. After many millennia of going through natural selection, evolving, destroying, and selecting their kind, our community came catastrophically close to opportunities created by inventive humanity to destroy all life on this planet and possibly Earth itself.

The second part of this book, *Homo Sapiens,* is dedicated to confrontations between two main political parties in the USA. President-Elect of the Republican Party, Donald Trump, was attacked and accused of different violations, from tax evasions to the Russian government's conspiracy. Trump was accused of having ties to the Kremlin, from which he allegedly could have been getting help during the 2016 election. All those accusations come from leaders of the Democratic Party who got the majority of the House of Representatives in the United States Congress.

BEGINNING

Today, not many educated people doubt that not only Africa is the cradle of humanity, specifically its eastern part. Discoveries by scientists are amending the history of the origin and development of other species of humans. New dates related to new findings and discoveries of remains of our ancestors go deeper and deeper millions of years back.

People inhabited the Denisovans' Cave in Altai (two hundred to three hundred thousand years ago). Some people who lived on Earth were genetically related to this mysterious population and lived on the islands of Melanesia.

Denisovan DNA has been found in ethnic groups in central Asia, southern Siberia, Mongolia, China, Japan, Korea, India, the Tibetan plateau, and further east in Melanesia, Australia, and the Solomon Islands in the Southern Pacific.

The theory of the origin of the apes, from which hominids developed, goes twenty million years back to one of the first creatures in the chain designated to a small ape called Proconsul. This tiny creature moved on four limbs, with a brain of 130 cubic centimeters. An existing opinion among paleontologists said that some other species might have been hominids' ancestors on Earth.

Numerous primate species were forced to settle in different parts of our planet, searching for food sources. Fortunately for us, the only one to survive to the present day was the species of *Homo sapiens*. Our species probably came across other types of primitive people living simultaneously. By luck or providence, the species of *Homo sapiens* won and survived to this day.

The first hominid is considered Australopithecus. The skeleton of a female named Lucy was found in Ethiopia in 1974. The age of this Australopithecus was determined at 3.2 million years. Evolutionists don't consider Lucy a direct ancestor of *Homo sapiens* and refer to it as standing "at the beginning of the branch, which developed parallel with the branch of man."

There is a common belief that apes ate fruit, lived in tall trees' crowns, and slept there. Trees become lower and fewer in the savannah because of climate change. Food searches forced the primates to move from one tree to another and stand on their hind legs, fearing possible predators.

Professor S. V. Savelev, like many other scientists, considers this version wrong and offers his vision of the transition of apes to direct walking on two legs.

In his opinion, twenty million years ago, eastern Africa had a warm and humid climate with many ponds and slightly salty water with many fishes, clam species, vertebrates and invertebrates, and sea snails. Much terrestrial aquatics, inhabited by fishes and flowering flora, attracted various bird species. Apes standing in water on hind legs were fishing in the water for food. They have to carry out whatever they can get, holding in their paws their pray.

BRAIN AND EVOLUTION

Humans inherited brains from our distant ancestors, primates. Our ancestors, ape mammals, came on shift after dinosaurs, possessed a multilayered cerebral cortex. Millions of years of evolution have made the brain of humans the most complex globally; this is the structure that manages all of our bodies. Different sections of the brain meet numerous functions of our body and dictate our behavior or desire. How does the brain work?

What makes us remember, think, worry, relive emotions, create new things, strive for perfection, or indulge in laziness? Scientists engaged in brain-physiology problems give us different, sometimes contradictory, opinions of the brain's functions. Our brains are not the most massive on the planet compared to such giants as whales, elephants, or even cows.

The brain of the modern person, in volume averaging 1,350 cubic centimeters, has lost almost 5 percent of its size compared to the brain of Neanderthals or primitive *Homo sapiens*. Reasons for such a phenomenon may depend on the history of civilization. Such losses could be associated with permanent wars and coercions into submission. Humanity must still find out how it could happen in the last forty thousand years of evolution.

These conditions, plus the influence of religion, suppressed intellectual freedom in the name of faith and belief in higher forces' help. It could have silenced the natural aspiration to fight for survival. Some scientists believe reducing the brain is a normal phenomenon because the volume of information in current life has density, and brains don't have to use the total capacity to react to it. Other scientists believe that such a significant loss of brain volume says something about profound negative changes that threaten the future of humanity's existence as a species. We are trying to understand such dangers, but we need to know how our brain is built. We don't have to worry or be afraid of the existence of ourselves or our descendants during peaceful times.

All connections from the central nervous system's senses come into the human brain—specific brain areas responsible for such functions. With two cerebral hemispheres, the brain is the ideal "command post." All the information comes in, instant decisions are made, and the necessary reactions to the changing situation are transmitted. Information on a new situation passes through practically instantly. Auditory, motor, sensory, olfactory, gustatory, and tactile organs transfer information to brain receptors. The central nervous system analyzes information and produces a responding signal. Then signals transmit through nerves to the appropriate body organs.

In the six-layered modern human's brain, two hemispheres of the cerebral cortex covered with furrows and convolutions and the associated spinal cord, there are neurons and blood cells in the nervous system transmitting electrochemical signals. Blood in the human body, consisting of liquid plasma intercellular substance, is reminiscent of the composition of brackish salty seawater. It contains different blood cells: red blood cells, white blood cells, and platelets. Blood is essentially an electrolyte that transmits electrochemical signals.

Neurons are nerve cells in the human brain that receive, process, store, and transmit information with electrical and chemical signals. According to various scientists, the number of neurons in the human body ranges from eighty to one hundred fifty billion. Neurons transmit signals to different neurons through sprouts to synapses. According to different scientists, the number of synapses in every neuron ranges from hundreds to a million. Moreover, synapses regularly destroy some connections and create new ones. Neurons provide nervous system functions—processed, stored, and transmitted the information. The nervous system responds to external exposure to the environment of the body.

Neurons form in the child's brain during the developmental period in the womb. After birth, neurons only increase in size, but we do not form new ones. Neurons that have died due to injuries, internal bleeding, or other causes do not recover. But some modern scientists believe differently.

According to S. V. Savelev, a Russian scientist, a doctor of biological sciences, professor, and head of the nervous system development laboratory of Human Morphology RUN—each human's brain is individual.

The surface of the cerebral hemispheres is covered with furrows and convolutions, more unique than fingerprints. But any brain has individual differences—qualitative and quantitative structural features. Differences between fields and subfields of the cerebral cortex hemispheres of the brain may vary up to forty times, and subcortical structures up to four times. Some subfields could be present in one person's frontal and parietal lobes but absent in others.

Significant selection variability of the brain turned out to be hidden in its internal organization. The brain of each person has different structures performing specific functions. The emotional, motion control, and continually changing associative tasks led to additional centers' appearance processing different information. Such an individual variability of the brains among different persons manifested by evolution as our species modified; naturally, it's just a long way, influenced by human civilization's history.

Nerve centers are responsible for different senses, movements, motor functions, and behavioral reactions. In large hemispheres of the brain's cortex are concentrated duplicate subcortical centers of the field, responsible for various senses and behaviors. Thus completing the vertebrate brain for millions of years.

The distraction of one communication—all chains associated with this brain structure—goes out of order. The brain is very vulnerable to different injuries, toxic impacts, or violations in blood circulation. Variability in the fields' sizes in the cortex, and, therefore, the incoming number of neurons, also varies due to brain mass. The brain in each person is unique. Differences in brain structures create insurmountable differences between people. Besides quantitative differences, qualitative differences are even more relevant to the abyss of misunderstanding between people. Even between loved ones and relatives, there is a difference in brain structure because it is not inherited.

Scientists distinguish between two aspects of human development. The first aspect—the evolution from generation to generation—and the second—human development throughout life. A newborn child has only the makings of human abilities. The child perceives social relations and learns to react like a human. Abilities become embedded in the cerebral cortex, in field size and subfields. Data from nature's capabilities allow one person to achieve a better result than others, requiring desire and work to form the personality.

The child cognizes this world, and the main factor in its formation is the social environment and the society surrounding him. From previous generations, participation in raising a child, the manners, customs, rules, and laws of society have been passed down. Sooner or later, the developing individual's brain will lead the person to the preferred occupation in which he will do better. The parent's task is to show a child the broadest possible aspect of human activities in many areas.

The study of the human brain has occupied enlightened humanity at all times. However, a more detailed study of the human brain began in the seventeenth century.

Phrenology—a pseudoscience—is the study of the relationship between the human brain's mental state and the skull's structure. Franz Gall, an Austrian doctor and anatomist, claimed that the human brain processes affected the skull's surface.

In his multi-volume work, Franz Gall argued that from childhood, physical and pathological specifics of a person's brain could be determined by examining the skull's surface—thus predicting its inclinations.

In the mid-seventeenth century, there was a widespread belief that the connection between the structure of the cranial box, body, and facial features connected with the psychological features of the person himself. The theory of physiognomy connects the character of a man with his appearance.

Phrenology and physiognomy arose in connection with the need for science to explain the motives of human behavior. The emperor of Austria, Franz I, forbade Franz Gall to give lectures. Franz Gall, rightly fearing arrest, fled to France. Phrenology remained popular until the beginning of the twentieth century. The development of neurophysiology has proved the theory of phrenology wrong.

The Russian Revolution, entirely unexpectedly, prompted Communist Party leaders to study the human brain. After the leader, Vladimir Lenin's death in 1924, prominent communists, including Felix Dzerginsky and Otto Shmidt, talked about the need to study the brain of the leader of the revolution, Vladimir Ulyanov-Lenin. They truly believed that his brain contained some special individual cells of genius. Those phenomena could be identified and then grow similar cells in the brains of the new generation. The new generation of geniuses could replace those with no place in the new communist world.

The country's leaders decided to create a brain research institute at the Academy of Sciences in Moscow, including a brain museum-pantheon foundation. The leader's brain could be exhibited to all progressive humanity.

The famous German anatomist Oscar Fogt was invited to lead the Brain Research Institute in the USSR. Despite the high foreign exchange costs, he brought assistants from Germany and his wife, who led the practical work with cuts to the brain. Most importantly, Fogt brought unique equipment, the equivalent of which did not exist in the USSR.

With Soviet assistants' participation, Lenin's brain, set in paraffin, was cut into several thousand pieces 0.02 mm thick.

In 1929, Fogt declared, "There are large differences between Lenin's brain structure and the normal brain structure." An article in the newspaper *Pravda* wrote, "The truth is it's an important contribution to the materialistic explanation of everything physical."

Lenin's brain was no different from regular brains at a volume of 1,330 cubic centimeters, with damage to the left hemisphere due to three hemorrhages.

The Institute for Brain Research continued its work, exploring famous scientists' and well-known artists' brains. Joseph Stalin showed no interest in the institute's work, and Fogt returned to Germany.

Works to study Lenin's brain were classified, as were those of Joseph Stalin's brain after his death in 1953; as we know, his brain was 1,330 cubic centimeters in volume too. Lenin's statement about Stalin is known: "He is not smart at all." A positive result of the revolution leader's brain study was creating an institution for studying the human brain that allowed Russian scientists to make many modern discoveries and get a new direction in studying the human brain.

Regardless, the idea of growing geniuses and creating the "Communist Society of the New Formation" died along with the USSR.

Those interested in studying the brain's functions can find many scientific lectures, films, and popular literature designed for the curious reader in various Internet publications.

Our task does not include a detailed description of the construction and function of the human brain. Such work is for scientists dealing with brain problems. We are interested in how the brain affects individuals and society as a whole and how the brain can change humanity by developing people's fate.

DUALITY OF CONSCIOUSNESS

People have fundamental norms of behavior. We all must make different decisions, from daily, mandatory's, and routine to complex and important decisions that could arise in our life path. Simple routine actions and decisions are made most often by instinct.

Instinctive: eating behavior, sexual, olfactory, defensive, reaction to sudden fear or environmental changes. All this results from aggregates of nerve structure and connections located in the oldest part of the brain inherited from our ancestors (primates), the limbic system—the part of the cerebral cortex located inside the cerebral hemispheres.

The limbic system is part of the brain's cortex, directly involved in higher mental and somatic (physical) functions. It provides behavioral responses designed to protect against emerging threats to life.

The limbic system, inherited from our primate ancestors, controls our behavioral motives related to our three primary instincts, particularly during puberty: food, reproduction, and the desire to stand out (dominate)—this system subordinates the early years of human life.

Girls mature at about the thirteenth year, and boys one year later. Behavior at this age in a social environment becomes unpredictable. Hormones, raging in the physical body, push for the most inappropriate actions. Falling in love and dramas experienced during maturation seem to be the most magical or the most horrific.

A fight between desire and necessity accompanies a person all his life. Hormonal passions can range from thirty to thirty-five years of age and much longer for some individuals. The limbic system inherited from our ancestors, primates, occurs in a small part of the human brain, about 10 percent; however, by influencing humans' behavior motives, capable of making someone crush the acquired rules of social conduct.

The duality of consciousness also makes people lead a double life. Practically everyone has something they feel is better not to show anyone. What is that? We call it the "skeleton in the closet." It's something hidden deep in people's minds and practically denied as something that could never exist.

Dual consciousness dictates behavioral motives. The survival mechanism offers adaptive ways in a specific environment, compromise, and cooperate. *Homo sapiens* seek a profitable and pleasant circle of communication and search for their place in the habitat. Conformism helps fulfill the primary mission—reproduction. The transfer of a genome to the next generation (create a family) made man furnish it with romantic, physical, sensual, aesthetic, traditional, or religious customs and often radical changes in fate. Creating the family indicates responsible and rational decision-making by members of the union. However, it's a consequence of our primate ancestors' vital instinct—reproduction.

Contrary to ancient instincts, the duality of consciousness allowed our species to survive in the wild and fight against multiple predators, other tribes, or cannibals. *Homo sapiens* learned to share food with others in the population, overcoming their instinctive desire to hide and eat everything by themselves. *Homo sapiens* overcoming this basic survival instinct could force the brain to obey the population's rules, eventually making them human.

The theory of the origin of hominids in East Africa, beginning in a warm, semi-aquatic environment with excellent protein content, has value. Naturally, the obvious question begs: weren't their predators there? Predators hunt everything that could be food, and our ancestors could be easy prey. Our ancient ancestors hoping for meals could be easy prey in the water, which was also inhabited by reptiles: crocodiles, iguanas, and varans. On the land, many large predatory felines prowled for food.

Giant predator birds flew in the sky and could easily pick up helpless victims, especially children, unable to escape or hide in the water. In addition to leopards and other large cats, giant snakes also hunted primates. It is more pleasant to swallow a naked creature and slowly digest it than to eat something like a deer with horns and hooves, which is more difficult to digest and takes longer.

Nevertheless, excellent nutrition and climate contributed to the reproduction of primates. Perhaps these conditions remained in the genetic memory of the higher primates as "paradise on Earth." We can assume that our species was lucky because not all of the species could survive, and many disappeared forever from the face of the Earth. Primates were consistently lucky, especially with many enemies and abrupt climate changes. Higher primates continued the struggle, allowing us, their descendants, to become humans and create a civilization of intelligent creatures living on this planet.

Why were primates destined to become human beings and populate the entire planet? There is an opinion that, for this role, individual species of dinosaurs could make a better claim. They had been around for millions of years. But they died out.

Humanoids began to walk upright, got a brain of 1,650 cubic centimeters, came out of Africa, created civilizations, science, art, and explored the cosmos.

How did we become human? What did we have to go through, and what is waiting for our species in the future? These are far from idle questions. Somewhere down the millennia, answers are stored on questions about the continued existence of our species, *Homo sapiens*.

What inspired an unremarkable primate species to transform from aggressive animals into intrepid discoverers of new lands?

They came out victorious against predators and, no less dangerous, neighbors; the same kind of humanoid who saw tasty and necessary food in those competitors survived by themselves.

Settling into the various continents, these future owners of the planet barely lived up to thirty-five years old, mutilated by diseases and predators. Nature also sent volcanic eruptions, cold downpours, glacial periods, and tectonic shifts. What happened there, so far in the past, and how did it all start?

Extensive excavations and research are bringing discoveries in anthropology (the science of human biological nature). Scientists tell us that the higher primates appeared in Africa about seven million years ago and settled in the continent's eastern part. Such data these days is updated continuously. An ancient primate species, well known as Australopithecus, had signs of upright posture and belonged to the group of hominids, predecessors of our species *Homo sapiens*. They were short primates, up to 1.5 meters in height, and walked on two legs. They had tiny brains—about 300 cubic centimeters. Australopithecus appeared about four million years ago and died out about two million years ago.

The following link in the chain is considered to be hominids, which have been called Pithecanthropus or *Homo erectus*. It was an upright species—the link from an ape to a hominid that anthropologists had been looking for a long time. Brain volume reached 950 to 1,200 cubic centimeters, and they may have made stone tools.

The climate in Africa changed to a colder one. Paradise's conditions turned more severe. The previously available and abundant protein food had disappeared, and it became necessary to fight for existence even harder.

Australopithecus was dying out everywhere, and a new group of hominids tried to adapt to the new survival conditions. Unlike the rest of the animal world, hominids did not have horns, thick skin, fur, fangs, claws, scales, or armor. Their only advantage was a large brain, which developed fast enough. Millions of years of being in "paradise conditions" with abundant and easily accessible food had allowed the brain to reach a size of no more than 300 cubic centimeters. Brain volume increase contributed by the struggle for survival, transitioning to eating the caloric meat of animals. Such a biological process occurred as a result of the struggle for existence.

Regular cannibalism allowed our species to improve and increase brain volume. Having a brain is the only weapon that has made man the master of this world.

THE EVOLUTION OF HOMO SAPIENS

There would be no happiness, but unhappiness helped. This one simple phrase could be an epigraph to the history of the appearance of our species. How did it happen that primates, with a brain volume already of 900 to 1,100 cubic centimeters, a species not having means of protection or attack, became people, masters of the whole planet Earth? They existed for millions of carefree, happy years, frolicking in the paradise-like climate of Africa. Yes, and they hardly would have wanted to know, even if they could think. Like other innumerable fauna species, our ancestors enjoyed the availability of various protein foods, with great pleasure multiplying in a society of their kind. They knew no other entertainment except for food and reproduction. They lived happily in large populations, which helped to fight others looking for gastronomical diversity.

But, as we know it today, our planet, like all cosmic objects, is influenced by the universe, and various cataclysms occur with it from time to time. One of these catastrophic disasters destroyed that familiar paradise world. The climate changed, and plentiful, tasty, healthy food practically disappeared.

The choice was simple. Survive by changing lifestyle or die. Most of the fauna died out. Our species, those who survived, searched for a place where there could be food.

They did not have any things for defense or attacks. They stuck together and went farther and farther, finding new places to inhabit for themselves (and for us). Such a constant struggle for survival pushed for activism, using the only tool they owned—a pretty significant brain. It contributed to their thinking and prompted them to survive in such a harsh, changing world. Now we know that our species, *Homo sapiens*, won this survival competition and inhabited the entire planet.

Living in primitive communal populations consisting of hunters and gatherers, group members learned to share food. This primary behavior led to developing areas in the frontal lobes responsible for such a phenomenon. There are no other creatures in the animal world that share food. We're not talking about the maternal instinct that makes the mother care for cubs.

Cohabitation, living in large groups, allowed them to defend against the attack and enabled a joint hunt for anything that could become food, including other representatives of humanoid species. Cannibalism was a natural lifestyle. Anyone who disobeyed rules established in a particular community could be expelled or sacrificed to a totem and eaten during a general repast.

People who reached an older age and became a burden to the community could also be eaten at mealtime. The pride leader tightly managed the flock family and established rules and regulations strictly necessary to follow. For disobeying, exile or death. If the pride leader got old or made mistakes, he could be sacrificed for the traditional meal. Such strict rules made members of the community obedient and submissive.

Submissive and easily managed members did obey, following established rules. It was then that the foundation was laid for changes in the human brain. Compared to Neanderthals or *Homo sapiens,* modern man's brain has shrunk by 50 to 250 cubic centimeters.

Large brain volumes developed as a result of a constant struggle for survival. It began to shrink due to the lack of personal initiative and obedience to ruling leaders.

Evolutionary processes by natural selection are the consequence of a biological people's socialized life in populations. For the history of human civilizations, which we count as more than five thousand years, natural selection continued—rejecting and destroying those who could not fit into a social community's rules. The certainty of following the community's laws requires participants to comply with all the rules and laws in any historical period prescribed by such a community or government. A different form of punishment for violation of the declared rules in city-states ranged in more modern times from general censure to prison time or even execution.

Religious intolerance led to this brutal selection, exposing the recalcitrant savages in the name of the merciful salvation of the mythological soul. Centuries and millennia passed by in the extermination of rebellious and dissenting individuals. World maps were redrawn continuously. New countries appeared and dissipated whole nations in a bloody crucible of conquest wars.

Nothing goes without a trace. *Homo sapien's* experience remains in the memories of the following generations.

The twentieth century brought two world wars and all imaginable horrors before which the cannibalism of savages—an innocent meal of a hungry animal—pale in significance. Not even the brain of a savage would have invented ways to burn and torment living individuals, the same kind, not for food but for the sake of their delusional racial or religious theories, multiplied by sadistic inclinations.

One can only guess what changes have occurred in the brains of each new generation born in such drastic times of wars and forced slavery in the last three millennia. What could trigger the loss of such a significant human brain volume? Several theories are trying to explain such monstrous acts of seemingly reasonable people.

Homo sapiens externally give the impression that we're just the same species. But it's outwardly, regardless of race and nationality. If we judge by the brain's construction, we are so different that sometimes we cannot understand others' motives and actions.

Bloody wars and cruel exterminations of different people, races, or beliefs occur because we represent different *Homo sapiens* species with different brain structures. How can we explain the behavior of one the most cultural nations in Europe in the twentieth century, with the unthinkable cruelty of primitive primates burning whole nations and poisoning them with gas?

Ashes from the burned bodies went to fertilize fields for higher crop fertility. Simultaneously, collecting railway trains with children's shoes, clothes, bags of hair, and torn-out gold dental crowns. And these were not individual gestures of sadists and executioners, receiving physical pleasure from the helpless victims' suffering. The Germans involved many other nationalities in this bacchanalia of bloody permissiveness. How can we explain the extreme cynicism and cruelty of the destruction of their people in Communist Russia?

African dictators/cannibals are causing doubts about the reasonableness of the human community. Can we accept Chinese hunweibins, bloody regimes of Pol Pot, Khmer Rouge, ISIL in the Near East, and terrorists of all specimens? There exists a theory that *Homo sapiens* could become bloodthirsty savages, blaming 2 to 3 percent of our genes inherited from Neanderthals and, at certain moments, dictate behavioral motives. This theory does not stand up to criticism because African leaders/cannibals don't have the genes of Neanderthals.

Another theory attributes insane blood bacchanalia's wish to inherit Pithecanthropus genes (*Homo erectus*), humans' distant ancestors. This species appeared in Africa about two million years ago. Many anthropologists believe that Pithecanthropus was among the first to come from Africa and settle throughout the Eurasian continent. There are findings on the islands and territories of Southeast Asia. They could be related to Neanderthals, Denisovans in Indonesia, and even possibly to *Homo sapiens*.

Pithecanthropus died out only about fifty to sixty thousand years back. There are finds of later remains, twenty-seven to forty thousand years ago. Most likely, they were cannibals and used stone tools and fire for cooking food. Russia's leading scientist, the doctor of biological sciences, professor, and head of the laboratory for studying the human brain, Sergey Vasilevich Saveliev, tells in his books and lectures about his vision of the problem of bad human behavior experience.

We had a long and cruel way of evolutionary selection from Australopithecus to modern man. We misunderstand physical causes associated with a lack of knowledge about human brain evolution.

Our species' limbic system logically explains individual actions and human society. The biological instincts that push a person to fight for his place under the sun at all costs contribute to the emergence of modern man's instinctive behavior—characteristic of the ape's past in the struggle for survival.

Through unification of hominids in society, the brain has been repeatedly subjected to pressure to select coexistence in a population.

To stay in a social group requires subordination and fulfillment behavior related to the community's adaptation to those who lead this community. Natural selection principles in the human community's long history led to mediocrity, and those who adopted such conditions have prevailed and succeeded. Individual initiative was punishable, but mediocre existence was encouraged. Those who stood out or refused to obey the rules of society were expelled or killed. In a primitive society, such non-adaptive members were probably sacrificed and eaten. In more modern times, we execute or imprison them.

CONQUERING THE PLANET

People who walk straight (Latin *Homo erectus*) or simply Pithecanthropus migrated from Africa in large groups, settled in Central and Southeast Asia, and, further, on Oceania's islands. They likely migrated to North and South America. In Georgia, a skull of Pithecanthropus was found dated to about 1.7 million years ago.

Sinanthropus ("Beijing man")—a species close to Pithecanthropus, had a brain volume of 950 to 1,150 cubic centimeters. They may have obtained and used fire, stones, and bone tools. More likely, they were cannibals.

Many scholars believe that several large groups of our ancestors migrated from Africa to the Near East and Central Asia. Some tribes went south along the coast of the Red Sea. There was a way to the southwestern Arabian Peninsula. One more route could be from the Horn of Africa through the Bab-el-Mandebian Strait (connecting the Red Sea and the Gulf of Aden) from 130 to 180 thousand years BC. Groups of people penetrating the Arabian Peninsula moved along the ocean coast, settling in India, Indonesia, the nearby islands, and further into Australia.

The super-volcano Toba's eruption on Sumatra, which happened 75,000 years ago, was the most catastrophic event in the last twenty-five million years. Damage from the eruption of Toba was astonishingly disastrous. It was a bottleneck for the barely-started human population. A million tons of volcanic ash covered China, India, Hindustan, the Middle East, and many other parts of the Earth. All living things were killed. The ensuing volcanic winter continued for six years. The population of Asia and Siberia almost died out. Earth experienced another peak of glaciation.

Heidelberger man (*Homo heidelbergnsis,*) a likely ancestor of *Homo sapiens* and the Neanderthals) is believed to have existed between 700,000 and 200,000 years ago. They used stone tools and probably fire and settled in Europe and Asia. Their brain volume was about 1,300 cubic centimeters.

In Africa, the changing climate, judging by all evidence, pushed people to search for new territories for existence. In Europe, the surviving Neanderthal population (*Homo sapiens Neanderthalensis*) adapted to the cold climate. This branch of people may have appeared on the European continent 120 to 150 thousand years ago. They lived in small populations and settled far away in the East. They were ancient, massive, chunky people with about 1,650 cubic centimeters of brains. They used fire and stone tools, made spears with sharp stone tips, and engaged in rock painting in caves.

About forty thousand years ago, tribes of *Homo sapiens* (*Homo sapiens sapiens*), our ancestors, with brain volumes like the Neanderthals of about 1,650 cubic centimeters, also appeared on the European continent. *Homo sapiens* survived, and the Neanderthals became extinct.

Numerous scientists have created plenty of theories and opinions about this fact.

Some claim that *Homo sapiens* ate their rivals; others suggest that Neanderthals were doomed because of a low birth rate and frequent mortality among children, which prevented this species from surviving. There is the perception that the Neanderthals' wooden spears were much heavier than *Homo sapiens*, and the *Homo sapiens* not only intercepted prey but could have won fights if any happened.

Nevertheless, Neanderthals have disappeared, leaving a footprint in our genes of 1-3 percent. Some people think that the reason for the disappearance of Neanderthals was that their diet was preferable to meat. *Homo sapiens* were omnivorous, eating wild fruits, nuts, meat, fish, seafood, leaves, and various plants' roots, contributing to survival. Over thousands of years, *Homo sapiens* have gradually inhabited all the continents of the planet, including North and South America. In addition to the harsh climatic conditions in their places, these primitive people, most likely cannibals, resisted various predators and other hostile tribes of cannibals, wishing to taste the new arrivals.

Hunters and gatherers roamed from place to place, looking for better food and living conditions. Besides the harsh climate condition, those primitive hominids fought others, cannibals, guarding females and small children.

The broad but undeveloped brain required fulfilling the three primary biological survival conditions humans inherited from our ape ancestors: food, reproduction, and rivalry. Food is a necessity for energy. In the absence of breeding, the species vanish. To dominate—a natural contest for superiority among their kind. Like many other species of animals that live in flocks, our ancestors existed in groups united by behavioral mechanisms. They lived in a large population—clans. The dominant leader could choose better food, the best female (or several), and require others to fulfill his commands and requirements. To dominate, the leader must be the strongest or the most cunning (with a weak populace). His authority must be indisputable, and anyone who encroached on his place must be killed, eaten, or expelled from the community. Such exile meant a death sentence since surviving alone in the wild, among the multitude of dangerous predators, was practically impossible.

Sounds were made into words, describing actions to create phrases and images. Sharing an exciting moment of struggle or persecution, hunters waved hands in motion, trying to convey what was happening.

Ritual dances and war-painted warriors still exist now. Probably then, during evolution, there was a need for voice communication. It required restructuring the throat, tongue, and mouth to create a set of words describing actions and items.

In the animal world, only humans have a form of verbal communication. *Homo sapiens*, moving from gestures to sounds, creating associative images of describing items and motions, made a gigantic step, becoming even more distant from their ancestors.

The use of fire finally cemented this gap. Humans learned to cook food on a fire, creating an external digestive process. Previous raw food intake, followed by prolonged digestion, extended the process. Raw foods, especially meat, also could be more dangerous to health.

What moved our distant ancestors to further resettlement into unknown and unfamiliar places (besides the changing climate)? The curiosity of pioneers, passion for something new and unknown? The necessity of finding new spots for hunting and gathering edible food?

More likely, it was a necessary measure to save their lives. Young and potentially dangerous to the ruling leader, members of the horde longed for freedom and opportunity. They could rise and rebel to persuade others to overthrow the power of the old one. All adult members of the community could kill the old leader. Another simple option was to capture a few females and go further into uncharted lands to establish new settlements. Each new generation could pass through such forced relocations. Resettlement of the whole planet went on for thousands of years; in the end, people populated the entire world.

Naturally, most of the population preferred to obey the leader's will and stay in the community instead of making risky attempts at freedom and uncertainty. Subordination guaranteed protection and some food, and fear of losing their established place in the population overpowered the desire for freedom. In society, an individual must suppress the freedom instinct. In such an environment, adaptive, compromise, and obsequious individuals survive.

KNOWLEDGE AND FAITH

It should probably be said that much new information and knowledge about man's origin and his resettlement across the planet are scientific achievements in all fields. Any educated person probably understands the evolutionary process that led the higher primates to today's "man of reason." It would be logical to assume that, possessing today's knowledge, a human will abandon religion and pay tribute to our mind, which helped us survive and subjugate atoms and space. After all, man has walked in space.

The brain of a primitive man, fearing the unknown and incomprehensible, created images of omnipotent forces capable of influencing the fate of every creature. Speech, which had barely appeared, made it possible to exchange concepts calling for deification and worship of unknown powerful forces. Belief in forgiveness in the event of a taboo violation or other misconduct. The certainty of punishment became the basis of behavioral motives. Not yet a religion, but the brain of a primitive man already used words and signs for reverence and magnificent worship with a sacrifice to higher powers.

With our advanced level of science and knowledge, being religious is somewhat naive today about the human origin. Passing off ancestors' superstitions as the true religion holds believers hostages of faith.

Together with that, the world's population will be approaching eight billion by 2020.

- Believers:
- Christians in the share of the population of the Earth: 33%,
- Muslims: 22%,
- Hindus: 15%
- Buddhists: 7%
- Jews: less than 0.2%
- Other religious groups: 2.7%.
- Non-religious: 13%

According to scientists, Islamic followers are outpacing Christians' growth and may become the dominant religion in the foreseeable future. When and how did different religions appear? What did religion give to the human race, and how did it affect us? Incomprehensible fears, like those of any living creature, lead to supposition based on a subconscious level. For many millions of years of existence, instinctive fear taught living creatures to hide, avoiding unknown (and therefore even more frightening) phenomena.

Natural disasters, drastic environmental changes, thunderstorms, falling stones, or trees inspired fear and awe. The hominids, learning to think, lived in a community/tribal horde because this was the only way to survive in those conditions, obeying the shaman leader's will. Submission to force and belief in the shaman's otherworldly mightiness helped the leader manage and rule the horde/family.

The earliest form of religion in primitive society was likely the animate mentor of the environment, wildlife, natural phenomena, and fears. Totemism and shamanism emerged, likely when primitive people united in tribal communities. It was more comfortable and safer for such groups to survive, given the surrounding predators and cannibals. Tribal communities were consistent with hunters and gatherers, united with the same belief in an assembly of mysterious spirits, threatening or helping to survive. A tribal leader could lead rituals and prayers to spirits relying on more charismatic and obedient members of the tribe leading religious rites.

Prayers, dances, chants, processions, gestures, magical spells, or other ritual actions were dedicated to mysterious forces. Such proto-religion existed for many millennia before emerging first civilizations began to build the first temples/ziggurats to worship multiple gods.

Different primitive communities chose their forms of reverence and service to spirits that could influence the community's life and well-being. It could have been a deceased spirit ancestor, sky, stars, sun, animal spirit as the ancestor of this community, natural phenomena, and other selected totems or fetishes. Such deities could be patrons of the tribe or exist as something threatening by their power its very existence. The deity would have been worshipped, sacrificed, and praised in chants and ritual dancing. Faith in the many spirits that inhabited the surrounding environments shaped the dominant and secondary worldview in the spirits' hierarchy. Evil and kind, helping and punishing, patronizing and opposing. Understanding and obeying all these plural gods bring good luck, health, sicknesses, or misfortunes took special people with specific knowledge to perform various ceremonies. Sorcerers, shamans, cult ministers, and the shaman's leader in the primitive community could combine all these qualities and use a group of assistant servants to perform ritual practices for primitive communities.

The shaman is a mediator between the community and the spiritual world. Belief in certain rituals performed by a shaman, and his ability to maintain well-being, avoid danger, or heal diseases would have been an early form of religious belief.

Primitive religious culture—shamanism—is preserved to this day among multiple nations, believing in shamans' mystical ability to travel and communicate in the world of spirits.

Ritual dances support the sacred status, chants, blows to a tambourine or other musical instruments, spells, and the unique *"shaman's trance."*

Shamanism is likely a religious culture that existed for many millennia before the emergence of polytheism's first civilizations and religions. "Specialists" of black or white magic survived the fight against religions and are currently successfully practicing among different nationalities worldwide. In modern religions, we can still find ceremonial rites preserved from shamanism.

Superstition is the basis of faith. Any religion is based on faith and myth. It does not matter what religion someone believes; it is still based on faith. Before becoming part of religious faith, all postulates and dogmas must be accepted unconditionally. In the first part of this book, we examined religion in much detail. It does not matter what denomination any religion is; it is meant to give a person hope for more than just physical life on this planet. Religion invents something holy and perfect into human consciousness, which humans must possess in all their life paths—the soul.

Flesh, the physical shell, is conceived in sin and continues to commit sinful acts in this weakness's strength, but the light, divine soul, atones for bodily sins. This soul is so fleeting and pure that no human sins can taint it. This divine gift is temporarily given for free use, and after a physical demise in some religions, the soul can live in another body because the soul is immortal.

All thoughts and aspirations of man should be directed to prayers and execution of all necessary rituals so that God believes in sincere remorse and a desire to atone for sins, made accidentally or involuntary.

Since a child is conceived in sin, they are guilty and must pay the price. To pray and correct this sin and many others (sinful thoughts, acts, unholy desires) requires repentance, fasting, prayers, and donations to the holy cause. Religious leaders dedicating their lives to a deity's service can help sinners find a path to correction. God will punish those who persist in sin through his faithful servants on this sinful land. Any physical punishment on this earth is not the worst one. Punishment is painful—torture, imprisonment, execution.

But the worst punishment waiting for sinners will last forever. For unrepentant sinners, just the thought of such punishment should make horror to anyone hardened in sins shudder.

Religion, even today, occupies a dominant place in human society. Traditions and religious holidays cause believers to gather for prayers and worship.

Thrill and excitement cover us during praying, like our ancestors during the howling of the shaman. Modern religious prayer in any faith is shamanism in its essence.

The next step of belief was choosing a single God. Those who know the Torah (Old Testament) remember how Abraham's grandson, Jacob (Israel), worked fourteen years for his uncle Lavan to earn the right to be married to his two daughters, then returned home with his wives and children. One of his wives, Rachel, took figurines of various deities she had worshipped in Lavan's house. They left secretly, without saying goodbye, since they feared they would not be released.

Finally, having realized that his daughters, son-in-law, and grandchildren had disappeared, as well as some figurines of gods, Lavan organized the chase.

The fugitives were caught, and Lavan rightly reproached his son-in-law for leaving secretly, not giving him a chance to say goodbye to his daughters and grandchildren.

For us, this episode is exciting because this moment was a frontier, marking the transition from polytheism to monotheism. Jacob, the grandson of Abraham, became the third patriarch after his father, Yitzhak. So narrates the Torah—the Old Testament (3,500 years back).

There was always a significant god in the pantheon of numerous gods. There was a single God in the Jewish religion, but before the Abrahamic faith, the main god occupied the dominant place in the hierarchy. Such gods were: in Sumerian-Akkadian mythologies—An(u) (father of the gods); in Buddhism—Buddha; in Egypt—the sun god Aton; in Greek—Zeus; in Roman—Jupiter.

In polytheism, there was a hierarchy of gods wielding power over various natural phenomena. In different religions, individual gods were responsible for different spheres of influence. According to the legend, gods rebelled against each other. They could have a relationship. The supreme god resolved contradictions arising between the gods.

The basis of any religion is mythology. Magic, belief in certain rituals and prayers, gave hope for fulfilling a particular request in the event of a benevolent acceptance of prayer and offering. To a particular deity must be brought the necessary offerings, accompanied by the specific prayers associated with the hope of fulfilling this deity's request.

Monotheism (belief in one God) has replaced polytheism (multi-divine) as the most progressive belief in a single living God, replacing the worship of dead idols of polytheism. It started about three and a half thousand years ago by the tiny nation in Mesopotamia called Jewish.

Judaism is based on believing in a single living God who created the whole world. This God cannot be seen or heard.

Moses received direct indication from God in the Ten Commandments carved by God himself on two stone tablets. His commands passed through the prophets he selected. As said in the Torah, Moses's five books were written by Moses in person during his lifetime (sixteenth century BC).

Torah, The Old Testament, is included in the Bible, the first five books. It is the teaching of the creation of the world by its Creator, God, Abraham's patriarch's history, the relocation of his descendants to Egypt, liberating the Jewish people from captivity, Moses's receiving the tablets of Covenant, and transition to the land's border, which God promised Abraham's descendants.

There is no exact date for when the oral Torah was first recorded. There are specific arguments that the written Torah appeared after returning the Jews from Babylonian captivity (third century BC). It is believed that the tablets of the Testament, kept in the Ark, were lost during the Temple's siege and destruction by the troops of Nebuchadnezzar in 586 BC.

The doctrine of Christianity canonized the Torah's texts, the scriptures, and the prophets included in the first part of the Bible.

By this doctrine, God is a trinity—God-Father, God-Son, and the Holy Spirit. This concept of God is reflected in the symbols of the Christian faith. This religion originated about AD 33 in Judea, connected with the teachings and life of Jesus Christ (Greek—anointed). Christianity arose as a sect of Judaism but soon separated into an independent religion.

Islam originated in the Arabian Peninsula seven hundred years later than Christianity. In Islam, Allah (Arabic—God) doesn't have a plural, and it's the concept of one God, the only one worthy of worship.

Islam recognizes the Scriptures, Taurat (Torah), the Prophet Musa (Moses), Al'iinjil (Gospel), and Isa (Jesus). The Koran was revealed to the Prophet Muhammad. Islam has many adherents around the world.

Similar religions (belief in the supreme deity) exist in Hinduism, Sikhism, Buddhism, ancient Egyptian mythology, Slavic mythology, Chinese, Japanese, and among adherents of other beliefs. Science cannot give any proof of God's existence. Such concepts as soul, paradise, hell, and holiness cannot be investigated. Evidence of the divine can be taken the same as blind faith (a truth that does not require a proof).

The right to religious freedom is one of the cornerstones of freedoms won by countless lives given for this right.

Religiosity relates to the field of the human psyche. Fear of the unknown, horror inspired by natural disasters, the inevitability of death, and the search for power to protect and give hope for salvation led humanity to religion.

Human weaknesses and phobias have forced the brain to seek the shield of higher powers and search for ways to contact the supreme, all-powerful deity. Religion is salvation from loneliness, support from despair, and comfort in tragic minutes. Hope is the foundation of religious faith.

After prayer, the brain injects into the human body hormones of happiness: endorphines, dopamine, and serotonin.

Such hormones are produced in our bodies when we consume certain products—chocolate, bananas, strawberries, and oranges. It is also possible to artificially increase these hormones of happiness in the body for medical purposes.

Monotheistic religions have banned human sacrifices and cannibalism and established a specific codex of values—kindness, love, helping others, family, and control over emotions and passions.

The religion established traditions—from birth to death, including festivities, general prayers, ceremonial rituals, and chants. Religion brought numerous brilliant works of art, architecture, painting, sculpture, music, literature, and science. Religion contributed to the dissemination of education and the creation of writing.

THE NEGATIVE ASPECTS OF RELIGION

Any religion has opposing sides affecting people's minds. Besides the mythology of formation, any religion is based on the faith's dogma. Once governing authorities approve, religion is intolerant to doubt or criticism of any postulate. Doubt is a sin. A sinner could be punished according to traditions, from fasting and penitential prayer to the sentence of deprivation of life. The sinner's guilt can extend to the direct "guilt" of sin to entire nations of "sinners" before God. The fear of inevitable punishment is sometimes worse than the punishment itself.

Religious leaders created hierarchical structures to control the flock and charge proper donations. Intolerance and a desire to subjugate as much as possible of the population led to religious wars and mass extermination of those resisting violent compulsion to adopt a faith. Such wars occurred at the dawn of creating the first civilizations and continue up to our time. Religious people are subject to severe influence. They do not need proof but hope for the forgiveness of invented sins. The manifestation of divine power would explain any phenomena that happen around them. Instead, lack of will, just living in the hope of God's help, is a consequence of belonging to particular castes ordained in the sacraments and making people submissive. Religion inhibits the development of sciences and the potential intellect of man. It is ignorant nonsense; not enduring any criticism or logical explanation does not require any knowledge. It denies learning in scientists and other knowledge unless they confirm the universe's divine building. Minds are poisoned by the drug of religious faith, plunging the brain into a hypnotic state of submissiveness. Such a condition can quickly transform into extreme fanaticism and aggression designed to protect its adherents' faith.

Instincts are incorporated into man through thousands of years of evolution. The dictate of faith orders people, fearing punishment or ex-communication, to obey regulations. Christian ministers of faith, whose psyche is broken by numerous prohibitions, suffer negative manifestations of suppressed natural needs and carry suppressed negativity to their flock. How many broken lives and ruined destinies, no one can count.

The human brain developed in the comprehension of new phenomena and concepts. We became human through the desire to survive in the struggle for existence. To overcome and stand against the cruel world in which people found themselves without claws, fangs, and nothing but the brain. That's made people the rulers of the world.

Suppression of will and fear of punishment for disobedience leads to the degradation of the individual.

The price of suppressing man's freedom, his natural desire to decide his fate, was incredibly high.

Human brain loss in a 50 to 280 cubic centimeters volume is more than substantial for our species. Millions of years of evolution let our species, *Homo sapiens*, become real humans with a developed brain of 1,650 cubic centimeters (same as *Neanderthalensis*.) Then the loss of a significant brain volume in a short historical period of forty thousand years makes us wonder about the causes of such catastrophic losses. Religious dictates significantly contributed to such processes, threatening unpredictable consequences for humanity.

Idols change, but faith remains the essence. Followers of Karl Marx seized power in Russia in 1917, overthrew the tsarist rule, and forbade any religiosity. There was no place in the movement for those who did not accept the new teaching of a bright future. Instead, people should learn to believe in the doctrine of Marxism-Leninism and the bright future of communism.

To many people, such radical solutions to religious problems seemed brilliant, and they were happy to join these preachers of new idols. Those who did not concur and escaped from the country were lucky. The others were waiting for a terrible fate.

After torture and beatings, concentration camps with hard labor could delay the time of death or a bullet in the back of the head. Many who served the new government and believed in the new religion could share the same fate as those who did not believe in a new ideology.

In Germany, Adolf Hitler, who came to power in 1933, opened a new religion, National Socialism, for Germans. An unimagined mixture of socialism, fascism, Nordic racism, antisemitism, ancient German Aryan mythological tradition, and German racial superiority over all other nations. The militaristic machine, powered by the mad Fuhrer, plunged the world into a terrifying war in the twentieth century. There was unprecedented inhuman cruelty, destruction camps, millions of dead, and humanity was thrown back for many decades, all due to a new faith. It was the worst nightmare humankind has yet experienced in its modern history.

In today's world, humanity is facing a new challenge. Radical Islamism has metastasized, scattering all over the globe aggressively and unapologetically. Islamism demands the introduction of Sharia law everywhere. They're ready for religious war. It will be much scarier than the power of the mad Fuhrer. Radical fanatics are eager to own nuclear weapons. Then it will not be winners or losers. All will perish. Radical Islamists believe in reward after death. Such war is impossible to win.

> *The fact that the origin of man from the animal kingdom determines that man will never be completely free from the properties inherent in the animal; however, the traces can only be about varying degrees of animality or humanity.*
>
> **FRIEDRICH ENGELS** *Anti-During*

> ... work changes a person's attitude to nature, and hence man changes in labor, through work.
> ... they (humans) begin to distinguish themselves from animals as soon as they start to produce the means they need to live... their material life.
> It is not the consciousness of people that determines their existence, but rather that their social being determines their consciousness.
> ... human beings are raw materials that cannot be changed in terms of their structure (e.g., a brain structure with a prehistoric time)
>
> **KARL MARX**

In his theory of reorganizing an imperfect society, Karl Marx suggested that all species' members have the same human brain. The task of the new society was that the organizers should separate and raise a new generation devoid of slave psychology, submission, and admiration for power. The new generation, free in spirit and free from the illusions of slavish cringing, will destroy the old world and build a new perfect world. According to Marx, it is precisely such a world, based on the equality of all working and free people, that will raise a new unknown force and turn the planet into a blooming paradise.

Unfortunately, at the time of creating his Marxist theory, humanity knew little about the human brain structure. Karl Marx's best assumptions were based on false notions of how the brain affects human behavior.

As we know, logic rules: "If the original message is incorrect, all subsequent provisions are incorrect."

Humans' brains are different and individual; we come from various species of higher primates.

Lack of knowledge about the brain structure and its features played a cruel joke on the founder of Marxist teachings. Based on Karl Marx's theoretical philosophy, the postulate of all people's equality did not consider the difference in people's brains. The diversity of races, origins, territorial features, and heredity made the individual human brain unique. Faithful students and followers of Marxist theory, led by Vladimir

Ulyanov-Lenin, inspired by enticing teaching, came to conclusions. The founder of Marxism pointed out a direct path to creating a heavenly future.

By Karl Marx's theory, it is essential to take power by force and destroy all who are the carriers of an ideology other than Marxism. After taking all the power, the next step is to grow a new generation and educate them by teaching Marxism. That generation then assigns a bright future society with equal opportunities for all people—communism.

It was clear that it would spill much blood and destroy unsuitable people, but there was the slogan: *Communists have the ability to solve any problem.*

To achieve universal happiness, communists have to ignite a world fire in which the old, worn, and useless society will burn down. This world will reconstruct the future's high society, for everyone will be equal and happy.

A peculiar Roman democracy led to the dictatorship of Caesar and numerous tyrant Caesars after him. The French Revolution ended in the dictatorship of Napoleon. Waves of numerous wars that flooded Europe ended with the catastrophic defeat of France. Many years of battles have brought redistribution of territories, devastation, and countless victims of the population in all countries involved in the conflicts.

The wounds inflicted by the National Socialist racial philosophy of Hitler have not yet healed, although seventy-five years have passed. The Marxists who seized power in Russia spilled seas of blood, drowning in them the best representatives of a nation, creating an authoritarian power that, for many years, passed into the oligarchic-officials rule, which practically destroyed a once-mighty state.

Marx's utopian theory in Russia destroyed everything with an elementary misunderstanding of the human brain structure by faithful followers of Marxist teachings. After many years, Russia decided to return to the market economy.

Josef Stalin ruled from 1924 to 1953, and the liberal democratic world applauded him in rapture. The builders of communism attracted hundreds of thousands of enthusiasts to abandon their backward homelands and race to the Soviet Union to help build a tremendous bright dream.

Flying like silly butterflies, attracted by the fire, they burned in an unthinkable fire raging on the vast territory of former tsarist Russia. The leader of the world proletariat, V. Lenin, died. After furious bickering over his place, a new leader shone over the devastated country for long and terrible years. As a result, it's all ravaged, cities ruined and the nation's most educational and best representatives destroyed.

The Gulag (a system of labor camps) regularly ground the intimidated, enslaved population, erecting monumental structures in honor of the leader so loved by people—communist Joseph Stalin. His time was up, and the bloody dictator was dead. His image still lives.

All new leaders worldwide, inspired by the idea of building a society of equal opportunity, use hypocritical power, where the population is voluntary slaves. The rulers destroy the people's minds and the subordinate the country's economy to extract maximum profits for the ruling class.

DEMOCRACY IN THE UNITED STATES

On the other side of the world's oceans, on North American soil, is the country where democratic principles, elevated to doctrine, are set out by the US Constitution. Democracy is a "sacred cow," and fundamental principles, pledged by the untouchable Founding Fathers, bloomed in lush color about yet another new religion—radical democracy.

More than half of the world's population are supporters of this seemingly right-for-all-times ideology. They like to be rich but also be in power. They believe that only such democracy is the essential faithful building of modern society and that all other formations lead to inequality.

Tolerance means acceptance of a different worldview, lifestyle, behavior, and actions. Postulate as a religion of the twenty-first century, a statement that does not require proof brings its adherents to extreme intolerance towards anyone who questions the legitimacy of the proclaimed ideas. The principles of declared liberalism take precedence over common sense. The right of people to express anger, crushing and destroying everything around them, is not perceived as violence for radical democrats. Rejection of family values, intervention in the upbringing of the younger generation, sexual freedom, and the rejection of the usual concepts of genders are goals of new rebels. Tolerance for the oppressed and fierce hatred for those who do not share these values can destroy the generation's most significant achievements. Radical destroyers are already in power, democratically elected. They love it, and they wish to keep it this way.

Humanity, in its history, has repeatedly passed through certain stages in its development. Something similar happened in ancient Greece, the Roman Empire, and post-revolutionary Russia. The first decree of Soviet Russia was the state where criminal prosecution for homosexuality was abolished. There was a theory that "a glass of water," consisting of denial of love and relationship between a man and a woman to an instinctive sexual need, should be satisfied without any "conditions," as simply as quenching thirst. Decreed on the dissolution date of December 16 (29), 1917, it was possible to dissolve a marriage without justifying reasons. According to the decree on civil marriage, on children and the introduction of books-acts of December 18 (31), 1917, "The Russian Republic will henceforth recognize only civil marriages …", which meant in those years, the cohabitation of a man and a woman.

In the 1920s, the "Down with shame" society operated. In 1922, its members held nude evenings in Moscow.

In Moscow and Kharkiv, participants of processions walked the streets completely naked or with a ribbon with the inscription "Down with shame."

Liberal democracy has burst into power in the last two decades. It has long outlived its life in various guises—the political model is the cause of most people's current turbulent state in modern society. Conceived as a political model of realizing freedom and justice as salvation from tyranny, it is hostile to the structure and culture of current morals and rules of society. Freedom becomes self-will, and the desire to disobey generally accepted moral rules and values is declared the highest achievement of freedom. Evil is declared good. Democratic liberalism is insolvent and practically not working. The democratic process of electing power breeds a dictatorship of voters—in fact, the majority's violence against the minority. The citizens of a country, who care about a system of values, freedom of enterprise, protection of the country's borders, civil liberties, and the country's priority, and its citizens, will always choose the best candidate. Liberals always choose the worst one, defending liberal social values. Keep open borders, prioritize the distribution of free goods and medical services for everyone, even those who did not do anything to create those values in this society.

It seems that liberal Democrats are on the mission. They wish for total power in Congress to make crucial amendments to Constitution. They want radical changes. They dream about socialism. The new one, not as it was in Russia, but a much better one. They are sure how to do that if no one is on their way. Leaders of democrats understand that mission is possible only if no one interferes. But here is the Constitution with the duality of power. Founding Fathers realized that power should be under control by balancing branches of government.

The American checks-and-balances model between Congress and the president provides for a clear division of power between each branch of government, which can be checked and limited by the other.

The same political party could control Congress and the presidency; it still is two competing parties, regardless of who is in control.

The Republican Party in Congress will always control and oppose any attempt to change the Constitution.

For democrats, there exists only one way to control the government: to get rid of the Republican Party for good, then change the Constitution. Or maybe to destroy the country to the ground and then lead a new, revolutionary government that can radically change the country and society. At first glance, this is a wild and unreasonable approach, destroying the economy and the power of one's own country.

The democrats can make the only right decision for this seemingly insoluble task. If they do exist, the architects are not out of mind with such a plan. They're not fanatics or haters of the capitalist system based on private property and the pursuit of profit. Democrats realized they could not eliminate the opposing party's competition without destroying the established institutions in a given society. The elimination of competition and the changes in the Constitution guarantees total control over the country for many decades. And the economy and power can always be restored if you have power and, consequently, finances.

History knows similar examples of cardinal decisions to seize power. In 1917, in Russia, a small handful of Bolshevik communists, using the liberal part of society to advocate democratic changes in the country, used the financial assistance of the enemy, Germany, and plunged the powerful empire into the chaos of the Civil War and seized power. Total devastation, hunger, poverty of the population, the horrors of the GULAG, millions of ruined lives—this was the price for the adventurous thirst for power.

The great French Revolution of 1789, which changed the social and political system, led to terror, innumerable disasters, civil war, famine, executions, economic crisis, and war.

The world changes now, before our eyes. And not only in the USA.

Into whose "bright" head this "grand" idea came, the world may not know. Maybe the world will never know. There are many options: Barack Obama, Nancy Pelosi, Bernie Sanders, or some unknown "genius" inspired by revolutionary ideas drawn from the deeds of communist revolutionaries. What happened in the USA in 2021–22, under the leadership of the more-than-strange President Joe Biden, with the full support of the democrats, convinces society that there is a definite plan.

America got open borders, the economy's destruction, and high inflation pushed into recession. The social structure of society and racism is embedded in the legislation and state institutions of the United States. Excessive spending, the decline of military power, the reputation for the weakness of what was once the most powerful nation in the world, the criminalization of society, sexual permissiveness, and the propaganda of white guilt. As well as the mandatory teaching of CRT or Critical Racial Theory, according to which race is not biological. CRT is a theory about how socially constructed racial identities are intertwined throughout all our legal and social structures to create and reinforce a system of white supremacy. Critical Race Theory destroys social power structures.

Republicans can gain a majority in branches of power, but populations of democrats are growing bigger for objective reasons.

The liberal democrats are fighting for open borders to attract the poor and uneducated. Sooner or later, liberal democrats will get total power—it's just a matter of time. Understandably, those people will vote for their candidates. The government's various benefits for poor people only created an unwillingness to fight for their place in society. In a low-income family, especially with a single parent, children are born to join the ranks of applicants for government benefits. It has been proved more than once by society itself.

Freedom of political struggle leads to society's stratification, those who create material values and others who enjoy these fruits. However, the latter requires an equal share of the earned wealth but also wants to be in power to pursue their vision of re-establishing society's rules. Liberal democrats winning the democratic elections become legislators pushing their laws in society. Combating this phenomenon requires a new political model based on the existing constitution, with amendments to address society's current situation.

The simple majority will always demand that they enjoy society's benefits for their well-being without doing their part to achieve this good.

The point of the political system of society is the common good. That's what laws are for, and officials must work for it. Accordingly, access to power should be given only to people able to see the common good and put it above the personal. They must not be in words but in deeds, prove their business skills, and defend the country.

The common good can be achieved if all society members have the same rights and responsibilities and are subject to the rules set out in society's constitution. It's the basis for choosing between trustworthy candidates. Two terms must be the limit to years in power instead of absolute terms. New amendments to the constitution must exclude random people selected by American society opponents and the country itself to get into power. Not just for presidents but both houses of Congress.

Any agreement will not resolve the opposition of those who want the freedom of entrepreneurship and private initiative to oppose those who want state control behind all forms of economic activity. No agreements or harmonization can resolve such differences.

Differences in the vision of state structure are bipolar and lead to aggression and open confrontations. Any social turmoil or revolution occurs due to unhappiness with the status quo, those who can not achieve success or position in society's social structure. In its failures, such individuals don't blame themselves but the unfair structure of the community. It is portrayed as the oppression of power. A given individual presents it as unfair to his talent and ability to create.

Opponents are exposed, severely criticized, and slandered. Sooner or later, in an unstable society, a leader confirms doubts about injustice in this community and calls for a violent overthrow of the existing authorities and establishing an equitable distribution of benefits among those who feel oppressed.

Such a leader is swamped with adherents, mostly radical youth, hungry for change. Unstable and exalted minorities join them, adventurers of all kinds, hoping to warm their hands on the burning fire, and those who could not, for various reasons, find their place in society. Like a religion, ideology doesn't require evidence, merely a belief in the right of those preached ideas. Divisions and injustices in modern society are the main issues. It is declared the first evil that must be fought against and united around the Democratic Party and its leaders—the goal for liberal democrats—is victory in the upper echelons of power. Liberal democrats announce that the existing government supposedly tramples upon values: "Taking advantage of a democratic system of the country, lack of equal opportunity, unfair distribution of goods and materials, lack of free higher education and free medicine." ???

Among other prominent human rights violations, the government is accused of racism, homophobia, xenophobia, the humiliation of minorities, religious intolerance, the arbitrariness of power structures, lack of concern for the environment, and many other sins.

Liberal democratic ideology finds many sympathizers in educational institutions where the younger generation quickly absorbs radical views and craves immediate change.

Teachers and students, primarily humanitarian faculties, study the history of Marxism with delight and believe that socialist failure in the whole world happened because of the wrong understanding and applications in the practice of such clear and simple concepts of total equality in building a socialist country. The media widely share ideas through show business, art, and culture.

The transition from a democratic to a socialist ideology was proven by senator Bernie Sanders, who is seeking the presidency's nomination as a Democratic Party representative. The vast number of supporters who voted for Bernie Sanders in 2016 and 2020 indicate that socialist ideas are gaining more and more supporters in American society. Adherents to socialistic ideas will lead their leaders to power to replace liberal democrats. With a high probability, we can predict that it is just a question of time when it happens.

Leaders of today's Democratic Party fear that such a radical party representative as socialist Bernie Sanders will only alienate those who are not yet ready to live in the socialist state. They decided to support Joe Biden, fighting for the candidate's nomination for the United States presidency. Results couldn't help but affect the last democratic primaries. Joe Biden got most of the electoral votes and became practically the only candidate willing to argue with Donald Trump in the 2020 presidential election.

It was unexpected and unpleasant for most democratic politicians when Donald Trump won the 2016 nomination. No one took him seriously because he was confronted by a heavyweight politician—the first female presidential candidate, Hillary Clinton.

The former First Lady under Bill Clinton's government, secretary of state, and a senator from New York; who would ever have doubted her victory? But it happened unexpectedly and inexplicably.

A newcomer with no political experience and a scandalous reputation won the election. Tragedy—that's how Hilary Clinton's enthusiastic and exalted supporters perceived it, and they decided to correct it in any possible way. Any democrats who shared democratic values and ideals united in a strong desire—to topple the hated new president-republican Donald Trump, by any means.

Democrats were well aware that the new president suddenly broke into politics; he undoubtedly represented immediate threats and danger. He is a wealthy businessman who doesn't depend on opportunities available with job positions and can destroy the established order in all the echelons of power. The decision to donate all his presidential salary to charity ($400,000) only reinforced democratic leaders' view in fighting this man who threatened the well-being of democrats.

Republican president-elect Donald Trump has come under attack and accusations from the Democratic Party. Democrats won the most seats in the US House of

Representatives. By the majority of the House, Trump was charged with Kremlin and Russian connections, who supposedly helped him win the 2016 election. Trump's answer was to promise to "drain the swamp," which refers to the Washington environment's corrupt officials' cleansing. He also said there was a "Deep State"—a conspiracy of power in all government structures. Such an intention aroused an immediate reaction.

The House of Representatives, in which democrats had a majority of votes, created a special prosecutor's commission to investigate allegations against President Donald Trump. Former FBI director Robert Mueller led the commission, named by Trump a "witch hunt," that spent two years of hard work and more than $40 million of taxpayers' money. The commission has been unable to find evidence of Trump's ties to the Russians.

Aside from the outrage, the troubling thought of electing Donald Trump to a second term of the presidency dictated a reaction immediately. The Democrats' hopes collapsed, and the anger demanded revenge.

There was only one choice. Remove the president from office under any cover-up. In the first case, Donald Trump was accused of connections with the Kremlin (a story based on the dossier written by a retired British officer of MI-6, Christopher Steele, and paid by Hillary Clinton).

Then the story of Hillary Clinton's relationship with Joe Biden, former vice president in Barack Obama's administration and now one of the democratic presidential candidates, surfaced. Attorney General William Barr received an official letter from one of the republican US senators asking to investigate Barack Obama's administration's involvement in Ukrainian politics and various strange ties to Vice President Joe Biden. Paul Pelosi, Jr., the youngest son of Nancy Pelosi, speaker of the House of Representatives (the leading opponent of President Donald Trump), appeared in a promotional video for a Ukrainian company. Nancy Pelosi's son in Ukraine represented that company.

The media broadcast this struggle story's overwhelming twists and turn in the upper echelons of power. It was more exciting than any film, book, or play. In time, the characters endured more than grandiose battles, smashing and crushing their enemies. Roman orator Cicero would have envied their sincere, heated speeches. Did they believe what they said? That is a curious question. But anger or resentment seemed to be very sincere on one occasion. It was a reality show about political life, more fantastic than *House of Cards*. Time will pass, and our descendants will appreciate the vicissitudes of this titanic struggle will go down in all the history books.

The battle was to preserve this country as it exists today or destroy the core and attempt to change its future history or even the world. Everything is happening before our eyes—we are all the extras on this landmark drama stage.

The liberal democrats, elected to the US Congress by democratic election, are currently the minority in the Senate Upper House and the majority in the House of Representatives. Democrats perceive members of the Republican Party as enemies and competitors. They are led not only by hostility but also by ignorance and evil. Hard to believe the cause of that ideological difference led to animal hatred for the current president Donald Trump. Loyalty to the clan requires, time after time, the president's crucifixion on the cross of impeachment.

The US Congress is one of the three federal governing bodies in the US. The US Senate, the Upper House of Congress, has one hundred members. Two senators from each state are elected for a six-year term. A particular rotation system in the Senate simultaneously takes the House of Representatives elections. The vice president of the United States is also president of the Senate. Only the Senate has the power to make the final decision in an impeachment process. Conviction requires two-thirds of the votes of the present senators. In this gathering, a majority of fifty-three votes belong to the Republican Party.

The US House of Representatives consists of 435 state representatives, proportional to the population in each state. Representatives of states are elected for two years and can be reelected unlimited times. The House of Representatives adopts federal laws, which the Senate discusses and are then signed by its president.

The head of the House is the Speaker, chosen by its members.

The beginning of February 2020 was marked by extraordinary events—scandalous processes caused by political disagreement. This undeclared war will go down in the history of America and will resound all over the world. The impeachment hearings of President Donald Trump continue. The third stage of the hearing has begun. The Lower House of Congress insisted on calling witnesses, including President Trump's former national security adviser, John Bolton, who House officials believe could be a key witness.

Donald Trump's "impeachment of the presiding act" (accusation) of the US Democratic Party's staging unfolded on Capitol Hill's world stage. The stage of the Lower House of Congress. They were directing and staging: Speaker of the House Nancy Pelosi; Chairman of the Judicial Committee Gerald Nadler; Adam Shiff, Head of the House Intelligence Committee. Could it be an act of despair or cunning calculation to discredit the president's reputation? Many politicians and reporters were guessing.

There was no real chance of the president's removal because the Republican Party has most US Senate members. Under the US Constitution, the Senate is given the right of the last party to approve or overturn the verdict handed down by the House of Representatives. The Constitution requires 67 percent of the vote, not a simple standing majority. It is clear even to Democrats that the president's impeachment will not pass in this scenario unless his guilt is fully proven.

Of what was President Donald Trump accused? In addition to the standard set of charges of "Act One" under the title "Mueller's Investigation"—ties to the Kremlin collusion—it doesn't matter that there was no evidence. Democrats believed there was plenty, but Mueller couldn't find it or didn't want to.

More than $40 million of taxpayers' money wasted two years of work and found nothing. According to democrats, the evidence must be there. After a lengthy debate, the democratic majority in the House of Representatives stood for two primary charges.

- Abuse of power (quid pro quo)
- Obstructing congressional investigations

So what was the abuse of power? The mysterious whistleblower said Donald Trump was pressuring the president-elect of Ukraine, Vladimir Zelensky, to use his position for his political purposes. In exchange, aid was promised to help, militarily and financially. It was said that President Trump demanded an investigation into the corruption scheme associated with the son of former vice-president Joe Biden in the Obama administration. Donald Trump has ordered the publication of a memorandum of a conversation with Zelensky, which confirmed Trump's request to find out the Biden scandal's details.

Trump asked the Ukrainian authorities to investigate Hunter Biden's connections in Ukraine. Democrats argued that it was all connected with the fact that Joe Biden is one of the 2020 presidential election challengers. Without any experience or knowledge in the field of exploration, gas production, or gas sales in Ukraine, and not knowing Ukrainian, Hunter Biden was taken on by a very corrupt company, Burisma Holdings—with a salary of almost a million dollars a year. In July 2019, Congress voted for the allocation of funds for Ukraine.

Trump instructed to pause military aid to Ukraine before talking to President Zelensky. The House of Representatives accusation was based on this fact, claiming that such a reprieve was made to pressure Joe Biden. Being Obama's vice-president, Biden demanded that the prosecutor-general, Schohin, who started investigating the company Burisma, must be suspended from work in Ukraine. Joe Biden threatened to freeze $1.5 billion in aid funds to Ukraine if Prosecutor-General Schohin were not fired within six hours. Many times, a video of Joe Biden making that threat was shown on TV channels.

Rudolph Giuliani, Trump's lawyer, former prosecutor, and former mayor of New York, stated that he has direct witnesses and proof of the democrats' collaborations with Ukrainian representatives to prevent Donald Trump's election in 2016.

`"There is direct evidence to prove the Biden family's involvement in bribery, money laundering, extortion, and other possible crimes."

In the House of Representatives, votes for the president's impeachment were divided by party affiliation. For impeachment—230 votes, against—197 votes, abstained—1. The Speaker of the House, Nancy Pelosi, decided to hold on transferring to the Senate impeachment case, trying to influence the decision and demanding the Senate explain "what will the process be like."

Donald Trump has announced four witnesses he demands to question in the Senate impeachment proceedings: former vice-president Joe Biden, his son Hunter Biden, the mysterious whistleblower, and Adam Schiff.

After all delays, documents with an impeachment resolution were submitted to the Senate on January 15, 2020. The lower house of Congress appointed seven representatives, *"Managers,"* to hand over material to the Senate on President Donald Trump's accusation. In this case, "Managers" represented the prosecution, the senators were jurors, and US Supreme Court Chief Justice John Roberts was sworn in as a judge and chair of the hearing.

The representative team of lawyers defending Donald Trump, Robert Wray, and Kenneth Starr are former special prosecutors in the impeachment case against President Bill Clinton. Alan Dershowitz, a former constitutional law professor at Harvard University, defended President Bill Clinton during his impeachment process. Two former federal prosecutors, Pam Bondi and Jane Raskin, spoke in President Bill Clinton's defense during the impeachment process. Also, everyone else involved in the process was sworn in.

It was the fourth case of the impeachment of a president in US history. First was the seventeenth president, Andrew Jackson. He was acquitted. The second case was the thirty-seventh president, Richard Nixon. He resigned in 1974 to avoid the procedure of impeachment.

The third was Bill Clinton, the forty-second president. He was disqualified from practicing law for lying under oath but remained president.

The first day of the meeting lasted fifteen hours. Mitch McConnell, the republican majority leader in the Senate, proposed a resolution to fast-track the impeachment, similar to that hearing held on impeachment for President Bill Clinton. The resolution was split along party lines (53–47) and approved by a Republican majority.

For the next three days, the House of Representatives managers read the charges to President Trump. From January 25 to January 28, the president's defense was speaking. Professor Alan Dershowitz's speech aroused particular anger on the part of the prosecution. The essence of this authoritative expert on constitutional rights (quid pro quo): "charges are illegal because the president not only had the right to use such an approach but was required by the Constitution to do everything he could to investigate a corruption-related crime against US officials."

The president's team of lawyers rejected all charges made by representatives of the House and called it "a dangerous attack on Americans' rights to choose president freely." As well as an "insolent and unlawful attempt to cancel the election results of 2016 and intervene in the 2020 election."

Senators voted on the prosecution's demand to call additional witnesses. A majority vote rejected that demand. Opponents of delaying relatively meaningless hearings, which can last long, justified their position because nineteen witnesses had already testified. The Senate asked about additional witnesses for the vote, and the simple majority spoke out against such a need.

The democrats were furious. They tuned in for a long fight, new debates, new pieces of evidence, and documents. All these efforts have been boiled down to reducing or lowering Donald Trump's approval ratings, blaming Donald Tramp for all mortal sins. The more lengthy procedure of impeachment, in the democrats' opinion, could lower the president's chances for reelection in the second term.

Donald Trump and his supporters set to end the impeachment process as soon as possible, preferably before February 4, when Donald Trump was due to address both houses of Congress with his annual State of the Union Address.

February 2, 2020, the main match of the season in American football took place. That's the most expensive sporting show in the United States, almost overshadowed by its political life. The average ticket price for this final match in the NFL reaches $6,390. Stars performing in the show included Jennifer Lopez and Shakira. For the first time, the Kansas City Chief became the champions.

This final match, the Super Bowl, temporarily overshadowed the battle over the president's impeachment. On Monday, February 3, the US Senate held the final hearing on President Donald Trump's impeachment. The final vote was supposed to take place on Feb 5, 2020.

On February 5, 2020, the Senate issued an acquittal on both impeachment counts. Votes were split by party affiliation.

One member of the Republican Party, Mitt Romney, voted alongside Democrats to accuse President Trump. According to the Constitution, collecting at least 67 percent of the votes is necessary to charge the president. Votes were distributed as follows; 52–48.

Following the vote, President Donald Trump was acquitted of both impeachment counts.

In Iowa, the traditional first caucuses for the democratic candidates for the presidency were held on February 3, 2020. The struggle for nomination in the Democratic Party finally led to seven applicants.

The two senators considered favorites in this race were Bernie Sanders and Elizabeth Warren. Up close to favorites was approaching former vice president Joe Biden.

Iowa's tradition of primary caucuses has kicked off the political calendar, fighting for the presidency. Officially candidates are nominated during the party's primaries. General statistics indicate that the winner of the Iowa Caucuses has a better chance of being nominated.

Iowa has less than 1 percent of the nation's population. Officially, candidates are nominated during the party's primaries. The outcome of the democratic Caucus has not yet been made public. The press service of the Democratic Party explains it through several technical issues. The unprecedented delay created many rumors. The Democratic Party was criticized from all sides.

Party leaders feared Bernie Sanders's victory since he had built his career as an independent candidate for many years without hiding his commitment to socialism. It could have been an absolute defeat for the Democratic Party.

Donald Trump tweeted: "Democratic co-stars are a real disaster; nothing works—just like when they ran the country." President Donald Trump won the Iowa Caucus of the Republican Party.

The Iowa Democratic Caucus' results came on the third day after the polls closed at Democratic

Headquarters. The final numbers were so unexpected that the DNC chairman insisted on a recount. Pete Buttigieg was the winner, with 25 percent of the votes. Bernie Sanders followed him with 24 percent of the votes. Former vice president Joe Biden rolled back to fourth place with 15.8 percent of the votes.

The following primaries were held in the state of New Hampshire. The "magnificent seven" of the Democratic Party were preparing for the courageous fight.

Pete Buttigieg, thirty-eight years old, former mayor of South Bend, a small town in Indiana, an Afghan veteran, an openly gay, likable guy, multilingual, and he is the main hope of the Democratic Party. As he called himself, Mayor Pete lives in his small town with his spouse, Chasten Glezman, and two dogs. Their same-sex marriage was conducted in the Cathedral of St. John in South Bend.

Socialist transformation supporter in the USA, Bernie Sanders, seventy-nine years old, is a senator from Vermont. He tried to run for president in 1976 and even outpaced Hillary Clinton, but then should have to yield under DNC office pressure. He professes Judaism.

Joe Biden, seventy-eight, is the former vice president of the Obama administration. In 2008, he tried to run for the democratic presidential nomination but soon withdrew his candidacy. But on caucus in Iowa, he showed meager results. Joe Biden is the Democratic

Party's hope for the 2020 election. On February 11, 2020, Democratic nominees in New Hampshire held the primaries.

Bernie Sanders won with 26 percent of the votes. After him, pretty close, with 24 percent, was Pete Buttigieg. Joe Biden fell far behind, with just 9 percent.

Donald Trump expectedly won the republican primary in New Hampshire. The party fully supported the incumbent president, with 97 percent of the vote.

The race for the US presidential nomination continues. Both parties battle for a presidential chair. The next stage in Nevada will take place in a month.

Another democratic candidate, Mike Bloomberg, joined the race for the 2020 presidential nomination. Forbes counts this billionaire in eighth place on the list of the planet's wealthiest people—with a capital of almost $64 billion. A former mayor of New York City, he was born in February 1942. In the election for mayor of New York, Mike Bloomberg was a Democratic Party member.

Then he moved to the Republican Party. He was re-elected to the post of mayor of New York three times. Founder of a financial market analysis and information company, he also founded the company Bloomberg LP, a computer network of financial news. The use of digital technology in media helped him master a new niche—stock trading online.

The debates of the democratic presidential candidates for the United States presidency in 2020 resumed in Nevada on February 19, 2020. From twenty applicants starting the race, there were only five left. Suddenly, with the help of the Democratic National Committee, one more democratic candidate joined them—Mike Bloomberg. Adding a new contender into the race caused widespread discontent among democratic presidential candidates. A barrage of criticism hit the new contender. He was reminded of all his "sins": unsuccessful statements in the mass media, accusations of arrogance, sexism, and racism. Despite spending his own money (more than $400 million), Mike Bloomberg suffered a straight defeat. Bernie Sanders accused the billionaire of "attempting to bribe voters."

Preliminary elections for the democratic presidential nomination in Nevada took place on February 22, 2020. Mike Bloomberg's defeat happened here. It was a failure, but not the end. He could continue to struggle for the nomination (especially as he was spending his funds) before Tuesday, March 3, 2020. This day is called Super Tuesday, when many states run primaries and nominations for candidates from the main parties to fight for the presidency for the next four years. Judging by past debates, Mike Bloomberg is not ready to fight and should decide what to do next. The most natural solution is to quit the race and retire (he is seventy-seven years old now), spending a billion dollars a year, maybe even two or three. Of course, he could switch parties one more time, but republicans, more likely, have already made their bet on Trump and will hardly want to tempt fate.

He could run as an independent candidate, which he's done before. He has plenty of money and has already said he could spend all of it to fight Trump. In the event of a defeat, he can go back and continue to fight. But what lies at the root of such hatred for Trump? They're both billionaires from New York. Publicly, they have exchanged friendly and respectful compliments at social events.

One of the billionaires' mutual acquaintances expressed an opinion on the reasons for their dislike of each other: he is sure there is "too much money and ego on both sides. Each one thinks he is smarter than the other, and he would have done better and more in place of the other."

Bloomberg decided to try to defeat Trump by pouring vast amounts of money into ads and his slogan, "Donald Trump trying to divide the country apart. If we wish the future for our country, we have to hold it together."

The recriminations poured in, to the amusement of the audience. Mike Bloomberg called Trump a "conman," hinting at manipulations with bankruptcy, and alluded to Trump's derogatory nickname for him, "Little Mike." In reality, Bloomberg is of small stature, and Trump mocks him for hiding behind the rostrum, which always causes public laughter. The struggle for the presidency turned into a real feud.

It must be said that the nicknames given by Trump to his opponents quickly stuck to them, and even the press reported these slightly offensive nicknames: Bernie Sanders—Crazy Bernie; Joe Biden—Sleepy Joe; Elizabeth Warren—Pocahontas (claimed to have the blood of American Indians); Adam Schiff—Pencil Neck.

Behind each moniker were the individual's typical characteristic features, particularly features of appearance or behavior—these unpretentious nicknames were liked by the public, who immediately recognized the personage. Democrats realize they don't have a bright and worthy presidential candidate capable of defeating President Donald Trump. Bernie Sanders, the favorite in the race, radically left, in fact, socialist, not hiding his radical beliefs, could scare away those still wavering about for whom to vote. Nomination candidates for the post of president of the country from the Democratic Party boil down to the following choice: The first socialist, Bernie Sanders; the first woman to be president, Elizabeth Warren; the first openly gay man, Pete Buttigieg; the compromised former vice president, Joe Biden; or the former mayor of New York, a billionaire professing Judaism, Mike Bloomberg. Not one of them has a realistic chance to succeed.

On primaries Super Tuesday, March 3, 2020, the Democratic Party, unexpectedly and surprisingly for many, brought Joe Biden forward. He was behind socialist Bernie Sanders in the race, but Sanders's statements supporting Fidel Castro's regime pushed him out of a wavering portion of the electorate.

Pretenders for nomination to candidacy for the position from the Democratic Party, one after another, get out of the race, casting their votes for the new leader—Joe Biden.

This turn of events suited the leaders of the Democratic Party. They were afraid of the unruly radical socialist Bernie Sanders. They did not believe in his ability to win the presidential election in November against a rival like Donald Trump.

A week later, there was another stage in the race for the democratic nomination, with Joe Biden again coming out as a winner.

The less time there is until the 2020 presidential election, the more intense the atmosphere will be. The struggle goes on for the chair of the country's next president. In reality, everything is much broader. Joe Biden is a representative of the radical left of the Democratic Party. His program was to raise taxes for the rich and increase government involvement in all areas. In foreign policy, a return to the principles of Barack Obama's administration. Trump's legacy is to be condemned and forgotten.

The Democratic Party has put everything at stake. The loss of the 2020 presidency could mean for democrats an unfulfilled hope for a prosperous and happy existence in many government branches, which implies the successful lives of the rising generation of their children and grandchildren and the hope that they will replace their parents in their time.

The democrats in the House of Representatives now have a majority and could lose it, which is a total defeat. Over the next four years, the triumphant unapologetic enemy, Donald Trump, will make so many changes that it is possible that a generation, or even two, may be required to bring back everything that was so hard-won during the Clinton and Obama administrations. The only logical choice—do everything to remove the president from power. As long as there is a legal majority in the House of Representatives, democrats must find compromising material and impeach the president.

The Republican Party has a bright, charismatic leader who knows how to fight and win. The main task—change the balance of power in midterm elections. Bring to Congress as many supporters as possible. That's not an easy task, but Donald Trump is self-confident. His brilliant performances during the caucuses and visible achievements in the economy, domestic and foreign policy, fighting the turbulence of COVID-19, and saving the country's economy, tip the scales in favor of the current president. If nothing happens that could interfere with his reelection, Donald Trump will remain for a second term as president of the United States.

Three years of Donald Trump's presidency have dramatically boosted the confrontations between the two main political parties.

The democrats, who won most House seats, have consistently orchestrated a real hunt to discredit the republican president. There was an investigation by Special Prosecutor Mueller, which turned out to be the FBI's operation. When this cart was lost, the democrats found a new accusation. They alleged that Trump was associated with pressure on Ukrainian president Zelensky to defame a democratic presidential candidate in the 2020 election, Joe Biden. Democrats had a majority at that time, and the House of Representatives voted for President Donald Trump's impeachment. The Senate ultimately rejected all charges and voted against impeachment.

President Donald Trump has to deliver his annual State of the Union address in front of the entire Congress. Vice President Mike Pence and Speaker of the House Nancy Pelosi presided over the event.

The moment was more than solemn. Into the House of Representatives, chambers entered senators, met with a standing ovation from the republicans, and a defiant rejection from the democrats. Some democrats were absent, expressing their protest against Donald Trump's speech. Female democrats observed the dress code as a sign of solidarity in the fight for women's rights, showing off white suits or dresses.

Before giving the speech, the president walked to the microphone and handed copies of his speech to the presiding official, Vice President Mike Pence, and House Speaker Nancy Pelosi. She held her hand to shake, but Donald Trump preferred not to notice it and turned to the microphone. Nancy Pelosi was visibly offended—as Speaker of the House and a woman. The moment was more than embarrassing and had consequences. Donald Trump couldn't forgive the excessive bullying and impeachment attempt prepared and pushed by House Speaker Nancy Pelosi.

President Trump's speech was as bright and impressive as ever. The achievements of the White House administration were very revealing. The country's economy is booming, and unemployment is shrinking markedly for all minority groups. Even more impressive is President Trump's government's success in foreign policy. Peace initiatives in the Middle East, bringing home American soldiers from war zones. In the last three years, seven million new jobs have been created. The government was rebuilding the army. The promises the president had given had been fulfilled—the stocks and bonds market rose 70 percent, adding more than $12 trillion. America became an independent energy country.

The president's brilliant and bright speech was interrupted a few times by great applause. Republicans met particularly vivid moments of the president's speech with tumultuous applause.

At the end of this joint hearing of both houses, the president's State of the Union speech was applauded. Speaker of the House Nancy Pelosi got up and defiantly tore up a copy of the president's speech, throwing scraps on the table. Her whole appearance expressed utter disdain and even disgust. Such a scene, of course, was noticed by all media. The next day, the press published this fact with many comments. They called her "Nancy the Ripper."

It is doubtful that such an unpleasant nickname will stick to an unlucky politician who lost to her opponents and somehow avenged herself, ripping up a copy of the president's speech in full view of the country and the whole world.

Over the past fifty years, events in the United States should make any sane person think about this country's future and the descendants who will have to live there. The political structure of the country's power, created by the Founding Fathers in 1776, has never been so shocked by a confrontation between branches of power. For almost 250 years, the checks-and-balances system has increased its prosperity and well-being, making the USA the wealthiest and most powerful country on the planet. History has left a sad trail of many countries and empires that seemed indestructible and eternal. Still, all of them were waiting for fate to be destroyed and forgotten over the centuries. Even the great Roman

Empire existed for more than a thousand years. The Eastern Empire (Byzantium) ceased to exist after the capture of Constantinople by the Turks on May 28, 1453.

The Western Roman Empire collapsed from the barbarian tribes' invasion, and the last emperor, Romulus August, abdicated in 476. The real reason for the Western Roman Empire's fall was that the assimilation of the barbarian tribes destroyed the country from within. They were granted Roman citizenship. Barbaric tribes did not possess the culture and ideology of Roman citizens. Differences in economic, political, religious, and cultural life developed into a crisis. Low birth rates among traditional Roman citizens and the high birth rate of new arrivals only reinforced this crisis.

Corruption in the power structures caused outrage and contributed to the emergence of leaders who called for rebellion and destruction. Moral decay prompted the flourishing of vices and evil.

Somehow, we can match these two systems, the Western Roman Empire and the USA today. Opposing strata of society, the irreconcilable difference in desires and intentions inevitably led to the state's social explosion and collapse.

The Founding Fathers of the US Constitution spent a great deal of time arguing over creating a long-lasting checks-and-balances system that would prevent the country from turning away from the democratic form of government and remaining an independent state. They created new principles in a political system designed not to allow any party to hold all government leverage. Most of all, they feared the possibility of dictatorship and, consequently, tyranny. They could not foresee such social changes in society.

Three branches of government:

- Congress
- President
- Supreme Court

These branches of government: legislative, executive, and judicial, interact, control, and balance power, guaranteeing the democratic legal base of the state.

Such a separation of powers enshrined in the US Constitution should prevent strengthening one of the government branches, ensuring the state's stability.

Two political parties control the US Congress. The Democratic Party stands for the government's influence on economic regulation and defends liberal values. The Republican Party is a supporter of conservative ideology and free enterprise.

Parties nominate future presidential candidates in the primaries. Campaign financing of presidential candidates is currently undergoing legislation adopted in the Bipartisan Campaign Reform Act of 2002.

Primary sources for financing the campaign:

- By private enterprise as well as individual benefactors
- Financial help from different types of groups (Political Action Committees)
- Finances of regional and national committees of parties
- Federal subsidies
- Own funds of candidates

Presidential candidates run in a general election across the country. Whoever receives the majority of electoral votes, at least 270 votes, becomes president for four years. The country's history had already seen cases when the presidency and Congress were controlled by one party. That can likely happen again during Donald Trump's presidency. He can quickly pursue his policies, seeking approval in both Houses of Congress. Such a situation means a complete disaster for the Democratic Party, who will do anything to prevent it.

Donald Trump could win the second term of the presidency. Democrats cannot allow this to happen. Donald Trump must be stopped by all means. So far, the House of Representatives majority belongs to democrats, and attacks on the sitting president will continue. The Democratic Party and the media are looking for clues to blame the president for sins. The well-beaten card is again brought to light—Russian interventions in American elections.

Democratic candidates are fighting for the nomination for the presidency. Democratic Party leaders fear radical statements that could push away hesitant voters. Primarily the Democratic Party electorate represents the most unfortunate part of society. They understand slogans and appeals from the democrats. All their troubles come from the rich taking a fair share of the profit from the poor. Choosing democratic candidates could change such an unfair distribution of values.

Democrat slogans: free medicine for everyone, free higher education, free kindergarten, guaranteed high and stable salary. For all this, it is necessary to raise taxes on the rich sharply.

The Democratic Party has noticeably moved to the left, looking more like the socialist camp leaders. Bernie Sanders was a leading democratic candidate for the presidency. He has positioned himself as a socialist, exemplified by odious figures such as Cuba's communist party, Fidel Castro, and the People's Republic of China Xi Jinping.

Such radical remarks, especially endorsement of Fidel Castro's policy, could scare voters and supporters of the Democratic Party. Joe Biden was hopelessly behind in the nomination race as a candidate for the Democratic Party. The fight between the two contenders for the nomination has entered crucial phases. With his revolutionary program, ardent socialist Bernie Sanders promised everything available for everyone and created the socialistic movement, enthusiastically supported by a fundamental part of youngsters, minorities, and believers in the Marxist theory of reorganizing society.

Suddenly, on Super Tuesday, absolutely unpredictably, majority voters revived a fading company and brought Joe Biden into the lead.

Socialist senator Bernie Sanders gave up the fight for the democratic nomination in the presidential battle. In November's election, Joe Biden remains the only candidate to oppose incumbent President Donald Trump. While Joe Biden has followed the closed regime, occasionally giving interviews on social media, Bernie Sanders has garnered many supporters with his socialist appeals: Everything is free! For everyone and now! Joe Biden has to reckon with many voters.

The USA is the leader of the free world, the rights, and freedoms of the people who inhabit it, the guarantor of prosperity and well-being for the rest of the free world. Now it could plunge into chaos and self-destruction inevitable during the battle of the revolution.

Did humanity learn the lessons of the bloody French Revolution? The destruction of the Russian Empire and the creepy "meat grinder" of *GULAG*? Fidel Castro's regime transformed Cuba, the pearl of the Caribbean, into a poor third-world country resembling Vietnam or Venezuela.

Cuba used to be one of the most attractive countries in Latin America. There were unscrupulous and irresponsible people who appeared, calling for storms and revolutions for the sake of a bright future instead reaping death and destruction.

America has always been a country of entrepreneurs. People whose private initiative created the wealth of this country. European settlers came to the New World in search of freedom. Religious, entrepreneurial, economic benefits, and opportunities. Firsts, colonists built their lives in harsh environments and struggled to survive—fighting indigenous peoples, royal troops, and diseases. The absence of civilization and state institutions' assistance has made this new nation strong, resilient, and independent. Freedom of entrepreneurship and private initiative made this country successful and wealthy. In a historically short period, the United States has become the wealthiest and most prosperous country globally.

Economic prosperity, political and religious freedom, and open business opportunities attracted to this country those who were not afraid of difficulties and hoped for their strength—with their skills and desire to fight for a better life.

In the nineteenth and twentieth centuries, big steamboats brought new immigrants, hoping to find their place in life. The booming economy demanded labor in factories, construction, plantations, specialists in all areas, and the service industry. There was a huge segment of the population that depended on entrepreneurs. The state took care of the social nature and measures to improve working conditions and the social security of those who worked for wages. The economic boom and prosperity required more and more workers. The administration encouraged immigration. Illegal immigrants got in and settled all over the country through a vast, practically open southern border. New arrivals a few years later underwent a naturalization procedure and became citizens of the country.

Latinos inhabited entire areas of large cities. Undocumented, they agreed to any work and for lower wages. Large families sent children to schools and used health services without medical insurance. The law did not allow people who sought treatment to be denied such treatment. Life in such areas increased the number of poor. Violence, robberies, drugs, and gang showdowns over such territories have turned these areas into hazardous places.

In addition to the many illegal immigrants, various minorities (a significant proportion of African Americans, the various groups from Latino American countries, Asian countries, and different groups from many other countries) represent a population dependent on state assistance. Such populations could not fit into the structure of the country. Especially for such groups, entire areas of social housing were built. Criminal enterprises quickly targeted those areas.

Drugs, alcoholism, and involvement in criminal business became the destiny of those living in such areas. Numerous assistance programs (welfare) only increased recipients' dependence, depriving them of the desire to fight for their place in society.

The Democratic Party's ideal electorate quickly succumbed to promises of immediate income redistribution and tax increases for the wealthy. Such promises aroused natural enthusiasm, fueled by clarification about the injustices of the capitalist system. This ever-increasing mass of unsettled and dissatisfied people threatened the established relationship between workers and employers.

Smuggling drugs, people, animals, weapons, and other goods brought billions of income to criminal structures. The country's open southern border practically became a loophole, which only the lazy did not use.

Until 2020, such an unsustainable societal situation and the slogans the Democratic Party leaders put forward pushed the country to a revolutionary transformation.

Millions of illegal immigrants employed in the country's shadow economy "off the books" sent back tens of millions of dollars to their families at home. In his pre-election program, Donald Trump promised to build a 3,100-km wall along the country's southern border.

The House of Representatives, where the majority represents democrats, refused to fund that wall. The Democratic Party has advocated for open borders and recognizing the right of illegal immigrants to vote.

Suddenly, the entire population of the planet confused all the politicians, affecting all life areas for almost everyone living on this planet. The political struggle has given way to a formidable danger that could forever change perceptions of the need for a more intelligent world structure. Humanity must possibly pass through the bottleneck of survivability in a catastrophic emergency, which will shock the whole world. A new unknown virus began its rapid spread from China, entered almost all the world's countries, and gave new energy to the democrats in Congress. They saw an opportunity to win back lost positions in voter confidence.

Trump asked Congress to approve a bill to allocate $2,5 billion in funds to fight the virus, in fear of requesting more than that in case of confrontations from the majority of democrats in the House of Representatives, led by speaker Nancy Pelosi.

The leader of the minority in the Senate, Chuck Schumer, stingingly critical of the president, has offered to allocate $9 billion. As a result, the House of Representatives approved the bill and allocated $8.3 billion. After Senate approval, President Donald Trump signed the law. The president, learning of such a significant increase in funds to fight the threat to the world, said at a briefing of journalists accredited by the White House, "Of course, we will take this money."

The world will have to pay the total price to fight this disease; no one has even imagined it yet.

CORONAVIRUS

What was, it will be, and what has been done, will be done, and there is nothing new under the sun. There is something they will say, "Look, this is new." But it was already in the centuries before us. There is no memory of the former and what will happen; it will not be remembered by those who will be later.

ECCLESIASTES

Translated from the Hebrew book *Kohelet*, part of the Old Testament outlined parables attributed to King Solomon.

While all the mass media discussed the ongoing battles of candidates looking for nominations from the Democratic Party in the presidential poll, the whole world appeared a formidable ghost of an epidemic called coronavirus.

Unexpectedly, the fate of the whole wide world intervened with "malevolent fate," which has repeatedly pointed out to the mind of *Homo sapiens* how fragile and ghostly its existence is. In the past, such an intervention of evil fate struck countless victims, showing humanity, the "hosts of the planet," all the futility and fuss of the struggle for life's benefits.

But other times have come. *Homo sapiens* are no longer so helpless and pathetic in the face of the challenges of a cruel nature. People were already aware of and preparing for the challenges of natural disasters. Of course, stupidity, meanness, carelessness, and sometimes malice never left the *Homo sapiens* species, bringing hostility, war, and tragic failures.

In February 2020, a new countdown to our world's fragile and imperfect order began. The country and the world were a menacing specter of the epidemic bearing the name COVID-19.

The World Health Organization (WHO) has named the new dangerous disease coronavirus. What is it, and from where did it come? First, it is a deadly viral disease. Many types of coronaviruses cause diseases when entering the human body. Any infected person is a booster of today's pandemic. The virus carrier is wildlife, such as monkeys, birds, snakes, rodents, and others. It's believed that the transport of the COVID-19 virus was bats. Giant snakes, rodents, pangolins, certain species of beetles, and insects in China are culinary delights and ways of established healing; there has been a belief for many centuries that such food helps heal. It has been assumed that bats or pangolins became the carrier of this particular virus, COVID-19. Probably there was an intermediary, for example, snakes feeding on bats.

Lately, more often, another theory of the origin of coronavirus is being heard. It blames some research institutions for viruses in China's Wuhan Province for intentionally or accidentally releasing a fatal disease. The world community still has to figure out the origin of this attack. We know that the virus came from China, from the Wuhan Province, where trendy markets sell wild animals for food consumption.

In China, persistent beliefs are spread about food that may cure certain sicknesses or general health problems. They use a meal of different types of animals and plants. Centuries-old belief in healing and recovery when eating such wildlife continues—nutritional treatments—ancient healing from different diseases. In connection with the coronavirus epidemic in China from January 2020, the government temporarily paused wildlife meat trading.

Then, China's government introduced a permanent ban on the illegal sale of meat from wild animals. The government is trying to eliminate the harmful habit of eating wild meat. The possible legal sale of wild animal meat, which brings multimillions of income, will go underground but obviously will not disappear. There is a consumer who is willing to pay more.

The virus has found its carrier.

The number of people infected with coronavirus worldwide is already counting in millions. The mortality count is up to tens of thousands. It is a highly aggressive type of virus, unknown to date, against which, so far, we have no medicine or vaccine.

Numerous voices are being heard demanding to punish the immediate culprits who put the world before the financial catastrophe. Numerous casualties, economic decline in almost all countries of the world, financial losses, psychological upheaval, fears for loved ones, and unclear survival prospects in the unpredictable future make the outside world unreliable and dangerous to create a family or survive. The unequivocal culprit of everything that happened is said to be China. Or rather, was it the Communist government hiding the virus situation from the world? In December 2019, it was already known in China that the virus was transmitted from person to person. In the year 2020, the Chinese New Year starts on January 25. The holidays in the country are from the twenty-fourth and will last around fifteen days. By tradition, such a holiday was used to gather the whole family. People traveled all over the country as well as abroad. Indeed, it contributed to the dissemination of coronavirus all over the world.

China's government blocked doctors' efforts in Wuhan to spread information about the new virus's infection risk. Hiding information led to five million people leaving Wuhan out of the vast city population of twelve million. The government banned travel within the country but not abroad. The infection began to spread all over the world.

Officially Beijing has imposed a quarantine on most of the country. WHO did not inform the world of what was happening in China. The world knows about large-scale epidemics coming from the East. A 1957 epidemic of Asian influenza started in China and killed nearly four million people.

In 1968, the same Asian flu was mutated under the name "Hong Kong flu" and spread worldwide. The epidemic claimed millions of lives—especially older people and those with weak immune systems.

In May of 2003, there was a threat of an epidemic called "atypical pneumonia (SARS)." Starting in China, in the province of Guandong, the disease, passing through Asia, spread to North America and worldwide. The Chinese, Singaporeans, and Canadians were affected. At that time, scientists knew that atypical pneumonia was caused by a mutated coronavirus passed from person to person and caught from a bat.

In 2005, a disease called "bird flu" came from China.

In 2009, China reported the emergence of a new virus called SFTS, or Henan fever. The name came from Henan and Hubei, where the disease was discovered. In 2020, COVID-19 infected most of the world's countries with a pandemic. Beijing began to send tons of supplies to fight such a virus in many affected countries. Soon these countries began to return said "gifts" because of their apparent inefficiency.

Numerous lawyers were formed to prepare indictments against the Chinese government, accusing them of concealing the epidemic's facts, resulting in a massive loss of life and economic upheaval worldwide. Various claims are growing up to twenty trillion dollars to be put up against China. Whether the communist Chinese government will prove its innocence or manage to get away with a less intimidating sum for the losses suffered—we will know only when humanity gets rid of this nightmare, the pandemic coronavirus COVID-19. Symptoms of this virus are like seasonal respiratory diseases resembling the flu or cold. Viruses mutate, so there is, so far, no vaccine or specific antiviral drug for this virus. It is transmitted by airborne droplets, as well as through touching contaminated surfaces. Some scientists say the virus could be transmitted through the eyes and even when breathing. Lately, the world has learned that the virus could spread not just by droplets but also could exist in the air and be active for a few hours.

What is this virus?

The opinions of scientists are contradictory. Some say this virus is a fragment of DNA-RNA, an inanimate broken part of an organism, such as a primary, not even a cell. It needs a cell to get into and then comes back to life and multiplies rapidly, infecting other cells.

Others claim that the virus is a living organism with its DNA or RNA capable of mutating, multiplying, and surviving.

It affects the blood cells and creates dangerous clots.

Viruses are the oldest inhabitants of our planet and are based on Earth's life, getting to us from space. From the way this virus enters our bodies, we do not have natural immunity. The virus can mutate. There is no universal vaccine for all viral infections. It will take a year or two to develop a vaccine against this virus.

Immunologists advise personal hygiene and caution, and simple safety measures. There is a danger of a second wave of the pandemic in autumn and then spring next year. An informed individual could provide security measures and prepare for any scenario. Fortunately, humanity has acquired experience.

Director-General Tedros Adhanom Ghebreyesus of WHO announced in early March 2020 that the number of coronavirus infections had increased thirteen-fold in the past two weeks, and the number of countries where the new virus had been detected had tripled. Therefore, according to his words, COVID-19 could be a globally dangerous health hazard.

Coronavirus, or COVID-19, is an infectious disease caused by a new virus that humans have recognized for the first time. This virus affects the airways, with symptoms like influenza. Prevention: wash hands with soap, wear a mask, and make minimal contact with other people. Numerous viral infection reports have been reported in many media outlets. It began in the Chinese city of Wuhan, Hubei Province, in late December 2019, when a disease similar to influenza's seasonal exacerbation appeared. But when it became clear that this highly contagious disease was very quickly transmitted from person to person and there were no effective medicines for it, the authorities sounded the alarm. But it was too late. The notorious globalization of the modern world, transparent borders, high-speed air transportation, and a passion for travel have spread with an unprecedented speed almost all over the world; deadly disease called coronavirus COVID-19. The virus quickly spread, and soon a fatal infection against which no vaccine or proven medicine was detected in most countries.

The whole world shuddered at the appearance of a menacing ghost of the epidemic, bearing the name of coronavirus, which made its adjustments to everything in this world.

Many scientists believed that the virus spread incredibly quickly to many countries. Following China, South Korea, Italy, and parts of other European countries went into quarantine. After prolonged hesitation, WHO finally declared the danger of the virus, COVID-19.

The World Health Organization has warned of the speed at which a new, dangerous disease is spreading. WHO's Director-General Tedros Adhanom Ghebreyesus, on November 3, 2020, announced: "The disease from COVID-19 can be described as a pandemic."

According to information cited by Ghebreyesus, the number of people infected with coronavirus in the world is 118,000 in 114 countries (according to other data, more than 4,200 people have died since December 2019. Italy (more than 10,000), Iran (more than 9,000), South Korea (more than 7,000), Spain (more than 2,000), Germany (1,800), France (1,700), and the United States (more than 1,000).

In the history of humankind, a pandemic has been declared only twice. The first was the 1918–20 grippe pandemic, known as the *"Spanish flu."* The second was the H1N1 flu pandemic of the years 2009–2010.

This emergency has paralyzed almost the entire world. One by one, countries announced a temporary suspension of existing rules and the closure of their borders. Donald Trump set up an impressive headquarters to combat the pandemic threat led by Vice President Michael Pence. For thirty days, the visits of European residents stopped. All US citizens returning to the country must undergo fourteen days of voluntary quarantine in their homes. All mass events: sports competitions, concerts, festivals, and parades, were canceled. Higher-education institutions were transferred to online education. Schools and kindergartens were closed. Like many other countries, Israel declared a mandatory fourteen-day quarantine for all arrivals in that country. The EU announced the closure of all its borders. Many EU member states have rebuilt their initial borders within the EU.

Fear has paralyzed the life of the whole world. The stock market collapsed, and this fall only continues. The economic losses of such a global collapse cannot be imagined. There is no cure or vaccine to stop the spread of this overly aggressive and dangerous disease. The only advice scientists give is to exclude physical communication with the outside world as much as possible.

On March 14, 2020, President Donald Trump, accompanied by members of the established headquarters to combat this hazardous disease, coronavirus, delivered a speech to the nation.

An emergency was declared in the country. Trump explained that introducing a US crisis would allow the Federal Emergency Management Agency to spend up to fifty billion dollars from the disaster relief fund to fight the coronavirus.

A plan with immediate measures to combat dangers threatening to destroy the free world's economy has been unveiled. The House of Representatives approved the president's proposal by a majority vote.

The financial market reacted sharply to the president's address but soon rolled down again.

Donald Trump has announced a partnership between the private sector and the government to create the conditions for rapid testing to increase the possibility of coronavirus testing as soon as possible. General managers of Walmart, Target, CVS, and many others have pledged to set up so-called "drive-up" tent laboratories in their parking spaces to test for coronavirus by car. After sampling for infection, everyone returns to quarantine, waiting for the self-testing results.

All states have pledged to set up headquarters to deal with the coronavirus infection's effects and to increase testing sites immediately.

All hospitals in the country should quickly create emergency plans to help the sick and increase their beds.

Google has created a website circulating information on testing locations. The FDA (the department issuing licenses for foods and drugs) has issued a permit to test for coronavirus.

How different events develop depends on scientists and those who will find a means to rid the world of this plague of the twenty-first century. Donald Trump said, "Our job is to stop this virus, an invisible enemy." He confirmed his decision to take the coronavirus test.

President Donald Trump took the test, showing a negative. Vice president Mike Pence and his wife took the test. The results were negative.

Britain has gone its way under the declared COVID-19 pandemic and expects to isolate people over age seventy, possibly for the long term, who have the highest risk because of their age. Delivery to their doors of food and medicine will be made. Minister of Health Matt Hannok warned, *"Fighting with pandemic will affect all citizens of this country."*

Unlike many countries affected by the pandemic, the British authorities announced full-scale quarantine measures. They decided to pursue a population that will pass through the "bottle-neck" of coronavirus incidence. They believe in isolating the elderly, hoping that most of the infected will suffer this disease in a mild form to get immunity. Most of the infected may suffer this disease in a mild form and thus receive immunity against the disease

Considering this new type of seasonal disease may be repeated yearly, the acquired immunity will be a kind of vaccination. The British government's plan has been heavily criticized for its lack of drastic measures to combat the virus and unnecessarily risky decisions that could lead to a severe epidemic in Britain.

The government announced the introduction of quarantine in the country. Prime Minister Boris Johnson was taking a test for a coronavirus infection. The result was positive. The British prime minister went into quarantine and decided to continue to lead the country from his residence.

At the White House, accredited media have been briefed daily by President Donald Trump's team on information about measures taken or prepared to combat the terrible disease.

The US Treasury Department has called for direct payments to Americans, including a complete plan to help the country survive the economic impact of the country's $1.2 trillion bailouts, as the coronavirus pandemic has hit taxpayers and businesses. This Treasury plan requires congressional approval. In case of approval, the first tranche of help, $250 billion, and the first set of checks can be sent in April 2020. The second wave of checks was planned to be sent by the middle of May, giving billions of dollars in credit to airlines, small companies, and different economic sectors.

The package to stimulate the US economy has increased to two trillion dollars. Most Democratic Party members twice rejected the package, demanding to add items related to the New Green Deal Plan ideas. The general condemnation and tough stance of Donald Trump, who refused to sign any changes unrelated to the economic stimulus plan, forced democrats to agree to allocate two trillion. The project was signed by President Trump and became law.

The FDA issued permits for drug testing on groups of volunteers. These drugs include some previously approved by the FDA: anti-malarial, anti-cancer, Ebola cure, and other medicines.

Express tests for coronavirus infection must be carried out everywhere. China, where the epidemic began and from where it quickly escalated into a pandemic, claims the disease's peak in China has passed. The measures taken have brought a positive result. At thesame time, China has been criticized for hiding the epidemic's size and delaying disease development data. Voices call for the Chinese government to be held responsible for the economic consequences of the pandemic. In turn, China offered the EU assistance and sent a contingent of freed medical personnel familiar with the treatment methods for coronavirus's mass spread.

Some media outlets in the United States talk about the need for a change in drug production's global redistribution. China produces 95 percent of the antibiotics supplied to the United States. The obligation to provide medicines in the country is no longer just common sense but a matter of national security.

The 2020 coronavirus pandemic will undoubtedly change the world as we know it today. Universal quarantine, if it lasts too long, will destroy the world economy and bring famine and devastation, the scale of which the world has not yet seen. Each country must decide which way to choose and what measures should be taken to avoid a repeat of the all-out threat that can virtually bring down the entire economy and put the country on the brink of extinction or total dependence.

Universal quarantine, if it lasts too long, will not only destroy the world economy but will bring famine and devastation, the scale of which the world has not yet seen. Hunger riots will not deter either the security forces or the army. Distraught with fear and hunger, vast masses of people will destroy everything humanity has created for centuries. Such apocalyptic assumptions are worse than the pandemic itself with its many victims.

Realizing the threat of an extended quarantine, Donald Trump has gradually transitioned back to the country's everyday life. He is thinking of calling a deadline in the next two weeks, April 12. This date still has a symbolic meaning. This day is celebrated as Catholic Easter, the day of the resurrection of Jesus Christ. Many opponents of such a decision, especially doctors, are heard. They warn that if total quarantine is lifted, a possible outbreak of the second wave will be even more dangerous, and the COVID-19 virus may kill many more. Opponents agree with the potential loss of life and talk about the collapse of an economy that threatens even more terrible losses for years to come.

The president and Congress must make a fateful decision that affects the United States and the world's population. For the first time in humankind's history, *Homo sapiens* must make the decision, facing a catastrophe of biblical proportions, threatening to bring humanity back to the Stone Age.

Later, taking medical experts' advice, the abolition of quarantine measures will be postponed until the end of April 2020. Even though the quarantine's withdrawal is being postponed, no one knows how safe it will be. They call for different dates for the possible period of quarantine. From the optimistic, mid-June 2020 to the pessimistic, it was postponed until the summer of 2021. The most incredible scenarios of saving humanity from a terrible catastrophe that can surpass influenza's consequences, the most massive pandemic in humankind's history in the early twentieth century, are offered. Then the victims of WWI itself reached twenty million people. The death toll from the pandemic far exceeded the official fifty million. In November 1918, the First World War ended. American soldiers were loaded onto steamships and went home to America. They brought the "Spanish" flu with them. The epidemic mostly hit youngsters. Immunity battling the disease causes a powerful and potentially dangerous reaction of the organism that kills the infection, simultaneously destroying the entire body. The enormous sacrifices and monstrous devastation of the First World War and the pandemic, accompanied by an economic fall, pushed humanity all over the world back for decades.

In the first months of 1918, the first wave of viral influenza passed. Mortality cases were at the level of seasonable flu. The second wave of diseases started in the fall of the same year; a third wave arrived in the spring of 1919. Mortality was terrifying. Some patients died the day after the infection. Many cities were locked for quarantine, as they had in the Middle Ages, during cholera, plague, or smallpox.

A century has passed, and it seemed that a pandemic of this magnitude at the current level of medicine was impossible. However, humanity learned from the pandemic. Governments have been creating plans to save the population in the event of a threat of similar catastrophes of planetary proportions. An international health organization, WHO, was established to address such problems, first as a division of the League of Nations and later as a Division of the UN.

Time will pass, and then the world will figure out who is to blame and how and where it began. There are still many questions:

- Why were we not ready to confront the pandemic?
- Is it the punishment of nature or the creation of human hands?
- What to save in the first place, the economy or the population?
- Who should pay for lost lives and a ruined economy?
- How are these losses assessed if there is a culprit, a person, or a country?
- Why have lessons not been learned from the epidemics of AIDS, ebola, influenza, and H5NI?
- Why did the plague, called the Black Death, kill up to 50 percent of the European population from 1346 to 1354?

With the COVID-19 virus, the elderly population and people with various chronic diseases seemed most at risk. Sooner or later, humanity will be able to cope with this pandemic. Implications for the world economy from the COVID-19 pandemic will be horrible. Small and medium-sized businesses could be at a profound loss. No governments have trillions of dollars to help recover impacted businesses. Credits also will not help. Even interest-free credit wouldn't help. It won't bring back workers, customers, visitors, buyers, or tourists. Very few will succeed after starting again from ground zero (more likely from a big minus). Many will lose savings, housing, professions, financial independence, and security in old age. Many people will lose their health forever. Losses of relatives, dear people, do not pass without a trace.

The April 1, 2020 date on the planet: infected—860,954, the death toll—42,368. (BBC)

The economic consequences of total quarantine worldwide are not yet fully understood. One thing is sure; losses will be quantitative, expressed in monetary terms, and qualitative.

The economy's globalization was convenient for the participating countries when products were bought from countries where wages were much lower, working conditions were incomparably worse, and environmental requirements were often ignored. The population of Asia, where most industries are concentrated, will be more than 4.6 billion people by 2020. The US and Western European countries, realizing their dependence on the production of a broad range of goods, will reconsider their plans and return the output of products, in any case, those that can make these countries hostage to manufacturers.

The pandemic has made it clear that skewed globalization leads to a loss of independence in certain goods and services. These are primarily: medicines, food products, weapons, the latest technologies, electronics, software, communication, technological innovations, and more. Consumption of goods, services, travel, and entertainment will fall.

One big question the world should have to keep in mind—what will happen to the economy when manufacturing moves out of Asian countries?

It may be necessary to abandon production efficiency for a more equitable distribution of goods. In such a case, government interference in pricing goods is dangerous. It may result in a partial abandonment of the market economy and the transfer to the state administration to create products related to the country's security. Therefore, the emergence of corruption schemes might happen in totalitarian states. New management mechanisms are likely needed to consider and correct such phenomena.

The market economy is governed by demand under the influence of the price mechanism. In a mixed economy, the government participates partly to the extent that a reasonable allocation of resources is necessary. The abandonment of globalization and the pricing policy within each country can lead to customs barriers and export taxes on goods and services.

Survivors of COVID-19 will be quite different people. Free and happy—probably. But cheerful and carefree—hardly. People will be born after this pandemic, and we wish them happiness.

The lessons humanity will learn and how they will affect our descendants' lives will not be foreseen. But there remains hope, well known to the die-hard.

CONSEQUENCES OF THE CORONAVIRUS PANDEMIC

The majority approves President Donald Trump's actions during the worst viral pandemic that unexpectedly fell on the world. According to social polls, 61 percent of respondents support the president's work "in a war with an invisible enemy," according to the president himself. A headquarters was set up to save the country from a danger comparable to the Spanish flu of 1918. In addition to the president and vice-president, doctors, scientists, military, and individual ministers joined the rescue headquarters. Daily briefings on the country's state, work done, and planned measures occur at the White House for the media. Unprecedented measures to realize all the country's resources have been launched to save the country's population.

Democrats, led by House Speaker Nancy Pelosi, understand that Donald Trump's victory over an unprecedented threat to the nation's lives and the economy would automatically defeat the Democratic Party. Of course, there is an opportunity to unite with the Republican Party and fight against such a formidable enemy. But democrats have alternative agendas and adopt a different plan. Nancy Pelosi has created a new committee with the power to subpoena those who should help investigate the president's administration's behavior during the crisis caused by the pandemic. Suppose any blunder is found, or it is possible to call any decisions of the administrative team a mistake, this committee will insist on removing the legitimately elected president with another portion of impeachment.

The Democratic Party, with the false ideology of democratic movements aimed at winning a seat in the upper echelons of power, will fail. Liberal democracy, preaching the false principles of unification of the "humiliated and offended," settled comfortably in the government's offices. Receiving more than a posh salary and all sorts of benefits is taken for life's primary mission, the arrangement for descendants to tidbits, where it is unnecessary to work hard, have the experience, or understand something. None of this is essential. Parents will ensure their children receive honor and respect, paying for their stay on the lists of corrupt companies worldwide in Ukraine, Russia, China, and Arab countries. Wherever cash injections are required, this could be generously funded by American money. Of course, the host country understands that without proper respect for the giver's hand, that hand can vote against such unruly countries. Such a simple trick, but it works every time.

> "Democracy is the worst form of government, except for all the others."
> **WINSTON CHURCHILL** *(1874–1965)*

> "Democracy means the rule of the uneducated."
> **GILBERT CHESTERTON, WRITER** *(1874–1936)*

> "Democracy is the least intellectual of all forms of government."
> **PHILODEM FROM GADARA** *(110–35 BC)*

> "It is difficult to say which form of government is worse before everything is terrible. And democracy is the worst because what is a democracy but not the aristocracy of scoundrels."
> **GEORGE GORDON, LORD BYRON** *(1788–1824)*

> "Under the rule of a homogeneous and doctrinaire majority, Democracy can be no less brutal than the worst dictatorships."
> **FRIEDRICH VON HAYEK** *(1889–1992)*

The economy after the coronavirus pandemic could be destroyed in all countries. The urgent need to restore the economy will accompany a food shortage and other essential things. Each country will have to fight alone, to monitor security and order in the country, shielding itself from other countries' impenetrable barriers. The danger of new infection will force them to close the borders effectively, move away from globalization, and produce medical supplies, preparing to deploy paramilitary formations with all the necessary equipment and personnel.

The Declaration of Independence by the Founding Fathers in 1776 and the US Constitution in 1789 served as shining examples of the world's freedom and equality under the law. Freedom and equality of all citizens are an integral part of the proclaimed rights.

In a new reality, as in times of war or pandemic, the country's governance must be restructured to meet the times' challenges. The notorious freedoms of assembly, marches, rallies, demonstrations, and anti-government communities should give way to a firm and reasonable provisional rule of the party most prepared for the rational restoration of a shaken society. Democrats, with their particular ideology of helping the world, with demagogic free state support, open borders for all comers, and other false slogans, are obliged to make their choice.

1. Support the new government in rebuilding the country
2. Must restructure the country's governance

Unprecedented in scope in the new world, the unexpected blow of a terrible pandemic created by human stupidity put the world on the brink of survival. In a panic, unprepared states rushed to the other extreme, similar to people's actions in the Dark Ages. The city gates were closed during smallpox, bubonic plague, or cholera, and today, many countries race to close their state's borders even faster. Those who can survive inside the enclosed space hope to acquire immunity against the next scourge, and a grateful population will be able to evolve further into the foggy future.

The modern world's problem is not only the transparency of borders, flying planes faster than sound, or the financial ability to travel comfortably on massive cruise ships. The problem lies in the heads of modern people. No one is ready to give up the magnificent amenities of the contemporary world. Refuse travel, cheerful gatherings on various occasions, restaurant gatherings, or in-house celebrations.

Food is not enough for everyone today. But it is somewhere tyranny or slumbering religious backwardness prevails. There is absolute freedom in a democratic society, with a separation of powers and a system of checks and balances. Correct, this notorious freedom has long turned into unbridled demagogic "human rights" anarchy, which created a farce out of the political struggle. The Democratic Party rushes to power through the liberal media, using the base instincts of hysterical, dependent, notoriously deceitful, vile people's social culture. Humanity has already undergone various forms of denial of society's regulatory system of behavior.

Good and evil have swapped places. Everything the Republican Party does is presented to society as terrible and dangerous, leading to the country's destruction and the degradation of an oppressed society. Conversely, everything the Democrat Party says and does, the pure protector of an oppressed nation, happens for the humiliated and oppressed.

All the successes of the Republicans over the past three years in politics, economy, finance, international security, energy, employment, military superiority, and living standards of the country's population are either hushed up or claimed to be the improvements of the former, Obama administration. All the republican administration's actions and the president are distorted and smacked down by the liberal media. The Democrat Party leaders hid, waiting and hoping the ruling party would make a mistake.

Then they'll scream as loud as possible at all intersections, "We warned, we talked to him, let's get him. Impeach, impeach, impeach!"

The Democratic Party declares and expresses, "We're the real hope for the people."

The country must choose whom to entrust with managing such a crisis.

Beijing has begun sending tons of medicines and supplies to fight the virus in many affected countries.

Soon, these countries returned these "gifts" because of their apparent ineffectiveness.

The world will change, realizing the need to be free from globalism to create a new independence level. Countries must become fully independent in food production. Their advanced medical care, the creation of medicines and equipment will allow countries to achieve independence from common diseases and future contagious infections.

The COVID-19 pandemic will change the world, if not forever, probably for a long time. The principal role at this moment should be the collective mind. A sense of self-preservation should suggest—to whomever one can trust in such a critical moment—all of it, not empty words. Everything the Republican Party did in such a critical situation must be promoted as widely as possible. Fighting is going on not just for today but for tomorrow. We must do it for the peaceful future of our children.

President Donald Trump announced new headquarters to exit from quarantine and save its economy in May 2020.

Humanity has not learned from the French and Russian revolutions' bloody upheavals—the First and Second World Wars' monstrous consequences. The modern war against a viral attack shows how easily it can put humanity on the edge of survival in an unreasonably short time.

As it is said in Russia, *troubles do not come alone*. This century did not know about cholera or plague riots. Another deck of cards was thrown onto the table. Cheaters play with a marked deck of cards: race, slavery, gender, feminism, minority, and sexual orientation.

COVID-19 splashed out onto the streets of America's cities, a sad and depressing part of society. Inspired by democratic leaders' support, people fought the police, destroyed property, businesses, rob shops, and passers-by. Organized gangs, riots, loitering, fires, destruction, and banditry spilled out on the city streets. BLM's organized movements (Black Lives Matter) and ANTIFA led this "peaceful demonstration," turning cities into nightmares for law-abiding citizens. They destroyed monuments, burned police stations and cars. Crowds chanting "defund police" smashed shop windows.

These weren't spontaneous demonstrators. They were well organized, with posters, flags, loudspeakers, and formations led by leaders. All of it resembled Russia in 1917 or Germany in 1933.

More on that in the next book.

GRATITUDE

In work on this book used materials published in the media, public lecturers, debates of candidates participating in the US election campaigns, politicians' speeches, and scientists. Also, various sources of information are widely available in the public domain.

The first chapter of this book focuses on the Russian scientist's research and writings, doctor of biological sciences, Professor Savelev Sergey Vyacheslavovich. All rights to these printed works belong to the publishing house VEDI. Professor S. V. Saveliev is a paleo neurologist, evolutionist, head of the Russian Academy of Sciences human nervous system morphology laboratory. The author of numerous books, lectures, and speeches on radio and television, a scientist with comprehensive knowledge, devoted his life to studying the human brain. His modern ideas, the implacable position of defending his own, somewhat bold and innovative thoughts about today's society. Besides many fans, his words brought him many opponents and critics. The causes led to the loss of a modern man's brain volume of an average of 50 to 280 cubic centimeters.

Courtesy of VEDI Publishing
2023